FOR THE WIN

FOR THE WIN

CelebrityPress®
Winter Park, Florida

CONTENTS

CHAPTER 1

DREAM BIG, NEVER QUIT

BY D. "RUDY" RUETTIGER

RUDY RUETTIGER'S KEY TO ACHIEVING YOUR GOALS AND LIVING A BIG LIFE

As a kid growing up in Joliet, Illinois, I never thought I was special. I was one of fourteen brothers and sisters, born into a working-class family in a working-class neighborhood. Almost no one I knew went to college. In my neighborhood, you finished high school, found a stable, good-paying job, and lived a quiet, "normal" life.

People didn't expect much from Rudy Ruettiger. From an early age, I struggled in school. I would find out much later that I suffered from dyslexia, which made it difficult for me to read, do math, and understand my lessons. But at the time, my teachers wrote me off as "stupid," "below average." They gave their time and attention to brighter students. College was reserved for these high achievers, the kids with A's and B's, the kids with good SAT scores. I graduated third in my senior class . . . from the bottom. There would be no college for me.

On the football field, I lacked the size and the talent to be a top player. To be honest, I didn't like playing football all that much. What I loved was being on a team, doing my part, helping my teammates succeed. I loved the feeling of being part of something bigger than myself.

So how did someone like me—who struggled in school, didn't come from money, was short in stature and not athletically gifted—how did I attend Notre Dame University and play football on the same team that launched legends like Joe Montana and Knut Rockne? How was I able to take my story and turn it into one of the best-loved sports movies of all time—*Rudy*? How did I build a charity that helps kids all over America pursue their wildest dreams? How have I seen all of my dreams come true?

The ultimate key to achieving everything you want in life, regardless of your circumstances, is your mindset. With the right mindset, you can reach any goal and live as big a life as you choose.

ALWAYS HAVE A DREAM

For me, everything good that has happened in my life started out as a crazy idea, a wild, unlikely dream. If you want to achieve happiness, fulfillment, and success, you have to begin with a dream. Visualize yourself fulfilling it, imagine what your life will be like once you achieve it, allow yourself to get excited about it. Excitement, enthusiasm, and passion will draw people to you and will help you overcome any obstacles you face.

I was named after my father, Daniel, but there were so many of us Ruettigers that everyone in our neighborhood just called all of us boys "Rudy". When you grow up in a large family, teamwork is important. Each of us took on a paper route to earn extra money for the family. We slept four or five to a room. Our family motto was, "Work now, play later." There wasn't much room for dreaming or imagining a brighter future. My parents were conservative Catholics, and they raised us to be disciplined, hardworking, and structured.

Growing up, there were two constants in our lives, Sunday mass and Notre Dame football. It seemed like every Catholic kid in the Midwest dreamed of going to Notre Dame University. And the Notre Dame football team was legendary. In mass every Sunday during the football season, Father would update the congregation on the score of the Notre Dame game. I remember seeing how my father would sit up and take notice whenever the priest talked about Notre Dame. My dad, like most dads in Joliet, loved football.

After mass, we would come home to watch the broadcast of the Notre Dame game on our black and white television. My dad was a loving man who worked three jobs to support his big family, but he almost never smiled or laughed. Notre Dame football was his only real escape from the heavy responsibilities of his day-to-day life. Seeing my father light up at Notre Dame football games planted a seed in my heart. I wanted to make him as proud and excited about me as he was about Notre Dame football. I thought that if I could just get onto that field with that team, I could make my Dad happy. It was a crazy idea.

Soon, that crazy idea turned into a full-blown dream. I imagined myself at Notre Dame. I fantasized about wearing that golden helmet and running through the tunnel onto the Notre Dame field.

Did I have the grades to make it to Notre Dame? Did my family have the money to send me there? Was I a high school football star who could win a scholarship to one of the greatest college teams in America? No, I had none of those things going for me. All I had was a crazy dream and the passion to make it a reality.

It all starts with your dreams. Don't worry about why your dream won't work. Don't worry about the obstacles. Don't worry that you don't have all the answers. Once you have your dream clearly in your heart, put all of your focus on how to make it happen. Act as if it is a done deal. Push your doubts aside and decide, then and there, that you will make it happen.

The next step is to seek out the people and resources that will help you realize your dream.

SEEK OUT PEOPLE WHO SUPPORT AND ENCOURAGE YOU

We all need people in our lives who help us, build us up, and encourage us to be our best. The second key to living out your dreams and goals is to seek out people who support you, mentor you, and cheer you on. Hang out with people who are a good influence on you and have faith in you.

When I was growing up, I didn't get much encouragement from the adults in my life. No one thought that Rudy Ruettiger was destined for greatness. But in 1969, I made a decision that would change the way I viewed myself forever, and it had everything to do with the people around me.

The Vietnam War was in full swing, and many of my friends were drafted and sent overseas to fight. I was a prime candidate for the draft. I didn't want to be forced into the service, so I decided to take charge of my situation. I enlisted in the Navy.

The Navy transformed the way I viewed myself. When you enlist, the Navy gives you a brand-new set of clothes; "new issue" they call it. As I got my issue, I thought to myself, *I've never had new clothes.* For my whole life, I had to share all of my clothes with my brothers. Whatever I wore came down from someone else and got handed down to someone else. Clean clothes were so scarce in my house that my brothers and I stole underwear from each other and hid it. So, when I got my clean, new uniform with my name stamped on it, my first thought was: *Nobody can steal my underwear.*

That uniform felt like a personal victory, and I folded my underwear, polished my shoes, and organized my footlocker with pride and enthusiasm. My drill instructor noticed. He saw something in me that no one else ever had—character, commitment, and a sense of pride. He made me the leader of my group in boot camp, and his belief in me changed the way I viewed myself. No one had ever asked me to lead anything before.

During my time in the Navy, another small encounter stands out as an example of why it is important to find people who support you. I was assigned to the USS Northampton, a communications command ship out of Boston. We were sailing back from Guantanamo Bay, Cuba, and it was my turn as helmsman. We were in rough seas, and one of the officers on deck ordered me to "Come ten left degrees rudder."

"Ten left degrees rudder, sir," I repeated. It was then I noticed that the officer was wearing a Notre Dame ring. I'd never seen a Notre Dame ring in my life. I'd never met a real Notre Dame man.

"Sir," I said, "did you go to Notre Dame?"

"Yes, I did."

My heart skipped a beat. "Sir, that's where I want to go when I get out of the Navy."

I'll never forget his next words. "You will, son, but keep steering the ship."

He could have put me down. He could have laughed at my dream. He could have been irritated with me for speaking to him instead of following orders. Instead, he told me not just that I *could* go to Notre Dame but that I *would*. And he reminded me to do what I needed to do in the moment and do it right.

There will always be people out there who do not share your faith and do not believe in your dream. Some people may make fun of you; some may try to tear you down because they are not living their own dreams. Avoid those people at all costs.

Seek out people like that Naval Officer. Learn to listen to the positive people in your life and ignore the negative ones. Following your dream will take courage, faith, and perseverance. Find people who will lift you up on your journey, who will help you along your path.

On the flip side, be a beacon of hope for others. We all have the chance to lift each other up, support each other, and encourage each other. When someone comes to you with a crazy idea or huge goal, fight the urge to tell them why it won't work. Tell them how it *will* work. Sometimes, even one encouraging word can change a person's life.

That Naval Officer probably doesn't remember me at all, but I will never forget him. His simple "You will" gave me the confidence to make my dream a reality.

USE ANGER IN A POSITIVE WAY TO HELP YOU OVERCOME OBSTACLES

Every one of us faces obstacles. We all struggle now and then to reach our goals. Sometimes the world is unfair and frustrating. Getting angry when things don't go your way can be a great motivator. Anger can fuel your passion and your enthusiasm. It can help you overcome fear, and if you use it in a positive way, it can move you closer to your dream.

It may sound strange, but anger has played an important role in my success. My high school teachers never believed I would go to college, much less play football for Notre Dame. My anger with them became a burning desire to prove them wrong.

Of course, I lacked the high school grades and test scores to qualify for Notre Dame, and after my time in the Navy, I was already twenty-five years old. My anger motivated me to find another way into Notre Dame. That way was Holy Cross.

Holy Cross is a tiny junior college located right across the street from Notre Dame. Its primary purpose is to prepare kids like me to get into Notre Dame in their sophomore or junior year. As soon as I learned that Holy Cross might lead to Notre Dame, I signed up.

I worked hard at Holy Cross. The Brothers and staff there discovered that my learning difficulties were a result of dyslexia, and they helped me to overcome them. I made A's and B's for the first time in my life. I knew in my heart that I was on my way to Notre Dame.

However, Notre Dame thought otherwise. While I attended Holy Cross, I applied to Notre Dame three times and was turned down—all three times! The third rejection letter made me angrier than I've ever been. What more did I need to do to get into this university?

The night I received my third rejection letter, I knew I needed to do something, so I took my dad's car and drove to South Bend. Determined to get some answers, I arrived on campus at eleven o'clock at night and pounded on the door to Corby Hall, where all of the priests lived. I intended to confront the provost, Father James Burtchaell, and demand to know what I needed to do to get accepted. The priest who opened the door thought, at first, that I wanted to enter the priesthood, but soon he arranged for me to meet with the provost, that very night.

It was almost midnight when Father Burtchaell welcomed me into his office. It was one of those big, intimidating offices, with rich wood paneling and filled with Notre Dame history and lore. I could feel the power of the place, but my anger kept me from feeling intimidated.

Father Burtchaell tried to explain to me that Notre Dame wasn't for everyone. Again, my positive anger allowed me to stand up to him.

I looked him right in the eye and said, "How can you say that? How can you say that Notre Dame isn't for everyone? Isn't it for people who want it and earn it? I just need to know what I need to do to get here. Tell me what I need to do, and I'll do it."

I applied to Notre Dame for the fourth time at the end of my second year at Holy Cross. This time, the envelope I received was thicker, and the words were wonderful to read.

"We are pleased to inform you…"

Anger, used in a positive way, can break down barriers and cut through red tape. I used anger to keep me going when I thought I might never make it onto the Notre Dame football field. I used anger and frustration to push forward in developing the *Rudy* movie. If you can transform your anger into constructive, positive action, you will be unstoppable.

NEVER QUIT!

I didn't attend Notre Dame until I was twenty-five years old. It took me nine years to go from high school into the Navy, then on to junior college and finally to Notre Dame. It took me ten years to get the movie *Rudy* made, including countless meetings, trips to Hollywood, and false starts. The time it takes you to achieve your dream doesn't matter. The important thing is to never quit, keep moving forward, seek out every opportunity, and have faith.

I believe that God would not give you a dream if you can't achieve it. My belief in my dreams kept me from quitting even when things looked their worst. If you continue to believe in yourself and promise yourself that you will never, ever quit, eventually your dreams can come true. My life is proof that dreaming big, surrounding yourself with the right people, facing obstacles head on, and sticking with it are the ultimate keys to winning your own game of life.

About Rudy

Against all odds on a gridiron in South Bend, Indiana, Daniel "Rudy" Ruettiger, in twenty-seven seconds, carved his name into history books as perhaps the most famous graduate of the University of Notre Dame. The son of an oil refinery worker and the third of 14 children, Rudy rose from the valleys of discouragement and despair to the pinnacles of success.

Today, Rudy is one of the most popular motivational speakers in the United States. It took years of fierce determination to overcome obstacles and criticisms, yet Rudy achieved his first dream – to attend Notre Dame and play football for the Fighting Irish. As fans cheered "RU-DY, RU-DY," he sacked the quarterback in the last 27 seconds of the only play in the only game of his college football career. He is the only player in the school's history to be carried off the field on his teammates' shoulders.

In 1993, TRISTAR Productions immortalized his life story with the blockbuster film, *RUDY.* Written and produced by Angelo Pizzo and David Anspaugh (the award-winning team who brought us HOOSIERS), the critically-acclaimed *RUDY* received "Two Thumbs Up" from Siskel and Ebert and continues to inspire millions worldwide.

"YES I CAN"

Today, a highly sought-after motivational speaker, Rudy entertains international corporate audiences with a unique, passionate, and heartfelt style of communicating. He reaches school children, university students, and professional athletes with the same enthusiasm, portraying the human spirit that comes from his personal experiences of adversity and triumph. His captivating personality and powerful message of "YES I CAN" stays with his audiences forever. Rudy's opening remarks receive thunderous applause and standing ovations from audiences of 200 to 20,000 people who emotionally chant "RU-DY, RU-DY!"

Rudy has appeared on various high-profile, nationally-televised talk shows and radio shows across the country; he is featured in national magazine publications, and has been honored with the key to many cities in the United States – with special proclamations for his inspiration, commitment, and human spirit. Rudy received an Honorary Doctorate Degree from Our Lady of Holy Cross College, the Distinguished American Award, a Proclamation from the Governor of Nevada granting an Official Rudy Award Day, was inducted into the Speakers Hall of Fame, and spoke at the White House during the presidencies of George W. Bush and Bill Clinton.

Rudy co-founded the RUDY FOUNDATION, whose mission is to strengthen communities by offering scholarships in education, sports, and the performing arts.

CHAPTER 2

THE GENIUS OF RUDY

BY "JOHNNY B" – JOHN BRETTHAUER

For decades, I've looked up to Rudy Ruettiger, Jack Canfield, Brian Tracy, Jay Abraham and many other Thought Leaders. I am grateful to have had the privilege of working with all of them on various projects. These are the bold ones, the outliers who pursue and achieve their seemingly impossible dreams.

Rudy especially fascinates me. He was too small to be a football player. His grades weren't good enough to get into Notre Dame. His family wasn't rich. He suffered scorn for daring to reach beyond his culture's accepted confines. As Rudy put it, "I faced a lot of challenges."

We've all heard Jim Rohn say, "If you want to have more, you have to become more." But how?

By standing on the shoulders of these giants, we can *all* reach higher. We don't live long enough to personally discover all the insights, strategies, and tactics our mentors have already mastered. At the same time, we don't need to endure the pain and waste time beating ourselves up because we can't seem to get where we want to go quickly enough.

Thankfully, these heroes have long been reaching out to take our hand and boost us even higher. With their help, we can avoid some painful detours and find the hidden reservoir of strength that makes our dreams possible.

WHY MOVIES?

Since I was a boy, I wanted to make movies that would be a force for good in improving our world. This is my global version of the Boy Scout concept of leaving the campsite in better condition for future campers—for tomorrow's children.

Great movies (and all art) move us emotionally. They define our focus and present a different view of the world—a world full of possibilities. Through entertainment, people can hear and truly feel new empowering thoughts. I want to inspire people (myself included) to become *more*, so we can all better pursue our dreams.

THRILLING SURPRISE!

I didn't realize that as a writer and movie producer I would get to personally spend time with my heroes. More than just photo ops, I get to interview them and share meals, drinks, and ideas. Because the vast majority of any film must be cut, I glean insights from outtakes, private meetings, and our talks to personally "get it" on a deeper level. This helps me to grow so I can bring higher value to my clients.

The more immersive and emotionally charged the experience, the stronger the impact on the mind and future behavior. These meetings are incredibly emotional for me and give me the ideal opportunity to more fully integrate the ideas these brilliant and empowering personalities so generously convey.

The time I spent with Rudy will enrich the lives of my family, friends, and clients (my extended family). I want to share these insights with you now . . .

DREAM BIG AND WORK HARD

Rudy was the oldest of 14 children. They lived in a small home while his father worked three jobs. Rudy and his brothers shared clothing and most everything else. He didn't even own his own underwear.

Rudy's mom encouraged him to dream and to dream big. His dad felt he should get a good job, work hard, and be a stand-up guy. Rudy's parents served as great role models for the keystone traits: Dream Big and Work Hard.

Life was hard for Rudy's father. His thrill was watching Notre Dame football. Rudy thought, if I could bring joy to my dad, that would be something. A dream was born out of his love for his father.

DARE TO DREAM BIG

After dinner with Rudy and the cast, and after the first day of filming, Rudy graciously allowed me a short interview. Thrilled to have this opportunity, I asked my wife to record it on my iPhone. As we stood in the lobby, an audience slowly gathered around us to listen in.

I wanted to know how he dared to dream and pursue such a lofty dream for so many years—especially considering he had no evidence whatsoever that his dream was remotely possible.

I wanted to understand the first sparks of Rudy's drive.

NUGGETS OF PERSONAL POWER

"Intelligence, hard work, and a sprinkle of good fortune are the seeds from which successful people germinate. Choosing to plow through the soil of fear and doubt by seizing on rare opportunities takes strength and courage. It is those defining moments that can transform a seedling into a giant sequoia."
~ Don Chiu, Sr. Manager, Mechanical Design Engineering, Tesla Motors

I asked Rudy what his core message is:

> Rudy replied, "Believe in yourself—that is the key. Once you believe in yourself, all the other stuff falls right into place. Nothing happens unless you believe in yourself."

> Like a hungry dog on a meat truck, I continued, "Where did you find that belief?"

> Rudy replied, "Your faith and your parents gave you that. And along the way, you find other people who kind of reinforce that through positive comments, like, 'Hey Rudy, way to go.'

> You keep collecting those little Nuggets. Hang on to the positive and *you let go of the negative* [see 'Goofy Thoughts' below]. You're not going to get them right away. You're going to get little bits at a time."

> [The key point here is:] *It's up to you to build it up.*

GOOFY THOUGHTS

Rudy knew where he wanted to go, yet he didn't focus on the details of getting there. It was easy for his friends and family to bust his chops.

As Rudy continued our interview, he said, "Don't listen to your Goofy Thoughts."

Rudy wasted no time on anyone's Goofy Thoughts, including his own! Instead, he collected Nuggets that built his confidence. That confidence built belief in himself and gave him the power to dream and make it so.

Action Step: Make a list of your Nuggets. Get your whole family to do the same and celebrate your victories by sharing your Nuggets. Build the power of belief in yourselves. And by all means, *Ban Goofy Thoughts!*

DREAM KILLERS/REVIVING A DREAM

Rudy graduated third in his class—that is, third *from the bottom.* He was an easy mark for anyone to make fun of, and they did. His teacher humiliated him in front of all his friends for his poor schoolwork. That's when Rudy began to let these Goofy Thoughts diminish his belief in himself.

Rudy said to me, "A Servant-Leader will never do that." But that was the adult Rudy speaking. As a child, he succumbed to the scorn and expectations of his culture. Rudy continued, "It is very hard to venture out of your culture. But dreams can be revived."

Eagerly, I asked, "How did you do that, Rudy?"

Rudy replied simply, "In the Navy."

FOLDING UNDERWEAR

In basic training, shipmates make their beds, fold their underwear, and shine their shoes. Rudy was excited. He knew he could do that!

Moreover, Rudy was grateful (gratitude is a Keystone Emotion), because he finally had *his own* underwear. No one could take them; his name was stenciled on the back! Rudy reflected, "You don't tell people about [your] personal victories, because they won't understand." Simply collect your Nuggets—your small personal triumphs. Who would think underwear would be a critical component of the Rudy story?

The drill sergeant noticed something different about Rudy and said, "You're a good guy. You're a leader of all these shipmates." Rudy thought, "Really? I'm a leader of men because I can fold underwear?"

How many times a day can you give a compliment for a job well done, no matter how trivial? In ten seconds, you might save or change a life by giving someone a Nugget of their own.

Rudy's attitude and all-out pursuit of excellence in this trivial task made him a leader. Excellent performance of today's (seemingly) trivial tasks builds your confidence and brings opportunities tomorrow. With a glimmer of hope, Rudy started to collect Nuggets again and rebuilt his belief in himself.

The Navy was looking for character, and they found it in Rudy, as we all have. Most people look for talent. But without character, it doesn't work. Rudy says, "Look for character and if the talent is there, then you have something."

FIND ANOTHER WAY

"When I look back at my life and reflect on my most successful moments, they have always been built on a foundation of learning from previous failures. When I had quick successes without failure, they were never long-lasting.

What separates the great from the good is the ability to navigate the uncertainty of life. In life, you will always face failures at one point or another, but the most successful people are not measured by their number of failures, but by the way they are able to persevere, learn, and rise from those failures.

I view failure as the fundamental foundation on which long-lasting success is built."

~ Jason Leung, Technical Director,
Samsung Electronics of America

In a stormy ocean, with Rudy at the helm and a lieutenant commander at his side, they were both seasick.

Rudy asked, "Is that a Notre Dame ring, sir?"

"Yes, it is."

"Did you go to Notre Dame?"

"Yes."

"Can I go to Notre Dame?"

"Shipmate, if you steer the ship, you can go anywhere you want."

"But I got bad grades, and I didn't take the SATs."

"You will find another way."

That's all Rudy needed: a kind word with a spark of hope to rekindle his dream and give him a Keystone Nugget.

This shows the leverage of a few words from a leader. We all have this power to change the lives of thousands of people as our paths cross.

LIFE IS TOO SHORT

Rudy's best friend at work kept saying, "Don't live in regret."

When his friend abruptly died in an industrial accident, Rudy heard his words echoed with a different kind of urgency. He quit his job to pursue his dreams.

Rudy said, "A lot of dreams are buried in the graveyard."

PASSION

"Have a clear mental picture. Visualize and dream about your success daily."
~ Doug Evans, Branch Manager,
Coldwell Banker #1 Office in Silicon Valley.

You could say Rudy was lucky. Each connection was tenuous and ephemeral. That's how life unfolds.

Rudy had a long-term focus on a single goal, and that physically changed his perceptions (Google: Reticular Activating System). This programmed his subconscious. He saw the lucky breaks that others would miss, and he took action.

Rudy positioned himself in the right places to befriend everyone involved, from the Notre Dame coaches, secretaries, dean and admission's office, to the students and even student government. He was on the Notre Dame campus so much that people thought he was already a student.

Rudy built relationships and shared his passion for his dream. That all-in passion against all odds is seductive. We all want to help that guy.

I believe Rudy is a genius. He had mentors. He knew when to listen, when not to listen, and when to talk back.

EVEN AUTHORITY FIGURES SOMETIMES NEED A LITTLE HELP

My favorite story that Rudy shared with me was one between him and a priest. Rudy dared to wake him at 11 p.m. at night. He desperately wanted to attend Notre Dame. Rudy said the priest walked over in his pajamas with arms crossed and looked at him.

"What's the problem, son? Come into my office." Then he continued, "Rudy, Notre Dame's not for everyone."

Rudy spoke softly with the power of a sledgehammer, "Really, Father? You mean heaven is not for everyone? Are you saying just special people go to heaven? That's not true." Rudy believes that God gives everyone a chance to pursue their dreams. He is a champion of the force of will and he has an uncommon intelligence to make his BIG DREAMS come true.

There is a lot more to this story... and it's in the movie *Rudy Ruettiger: The Walk On.*

Rudy said, "It isn't about *Rudy Ruettiger.* It is about *the story of Rudy.*" He said, "My passion now is to inspire others to pursue their dreams." And he has done so—millions of times . . .

RUDY THE HERO

Rudy said, "People don't care about how much you know until they know how much you care."

This sounded trite to me, until I really thought about it. My mind replayed a memory:

> I watched a hero fight back the river flowing through the breached levee that would imminently flood the town. He had no chance. It was one man against a river. But he worked with the determination of a man fighting for his life.

Inspired by how much he cared, how hard he tried, and the realization that he could not possibly succeed, the crowd rushed to work alongside him, and together, they saved the town.

I LOVE, LOVE, LOVE this trait of mankind—to challenge the impossible, to inspire and recruit the world to help make it so. That's just one of the reasons Rudy has such a profound impact!

The genius of Rudy is that in the pursuit of his DREAM, he asked for advice, ignored Goofy Thoughts, gave 100%, and amplified Nuggets. Rudy cared on a level that few ever do. And because of the relationships he developed with the students, players, coaches, managers, dean and admissions, plus his passion and massive action, people wanted to see him succeed. That's why so many people helped and celebrated his success!

Rudy created his own unique path (he found another way) using the resources that were all around him. And even in the darkest hour and after years of struggle—the tiny ember of his dream emerged into a flame worthy of a blockbuster Hollywood movie that still inspires millions of us.

WHY DO I PRODUCE MOVIES AND WRITE BOOKS WITH THOUGHT LEADERS?

So I can constantly improve by learning, applying, and sharing insights from the great mentors of our day.

My passion is to help my clients *keep making the right moves* and to help them *get what they want.*

It is my privilege to play all out!

Coldwell Banker
John Bretthauer Cal RE# 01480256

About "Johnny B" – John Bretthauer

Johnny B helps technology leaders in Silicon Valley buy and sell luxury homes. He is a Team Leader at Coldwell Banker. He is also a two-time best-selling author, speaker, media personality, and movie producer. Always keeping his clients' best interests in mind, Johnny B has earned the distinction of being a Master Certified Negotiation Expert, a Certified International Property Specialist as well as the designation of Graduate, REALTOR® Institute.

Johnny B was named one of America's Premier Experts® in recognition of his experience and success in real estate. This followed his appearance as a guest on America's Premier Experts, a television show designed to help the public make sound choices when buying or selling homes, filmed in Washington D.C., and aired on ABC, NBC, CBS and Fox affiliates.

Johnny B joined a select group of America's leading real estate experts to co-write a book entitled, *The Ultimate HomeBuyer's Guide: The Nation's Leading Expert Advisors Reveal Their Secrets of Success for Buying Right in Any Market.* On the day of release, *The Ultimate HomeBuyer's Guide* achieved best-seller status in six Amazon.com categories. In 2013, Johnny B was accepted into the National Academy of Best-Selling Authors®.

Johnny B also co-wrote *Success Mastery* with Jack Canfield and other successful professionals from around the world. This book also achieved Best-Seller status on Amazon.com. Johnny B's particular contribution, a passionate profile on how and why to harness the power of your subconscious mind, tap into *flow* states in business, and keep true to your inner moral compass no matter what, was chosen to receive the Editor's Choice Award. In 2017, he received a Quilly® Award in Hollywood for *Success Mastery.*

Additionally, he has teamed up with other best-selling authors, CelebrityPress® Publishing and the Entrepreneurs International Foundation, to become a Village Sponsor of the Global Learning XPRIZE® Initiative, a global competition to empower children to take control of their own learning and potentially lift 171 million people out of poverty.

Johnny B was invited by Realtor.com® to speak at the Annual RE/MAX

R4 Convention in 2014, and he received excellent reviews from numerous industry leaders for his insights into marketing and customer service in today's real estate industry.

His Bay Area radio show, *Real Estate Rumble*, was aired in Silicon Valley on KDOW and KNEW—to provide the public with real estate information and protection.

Johnny B's hobbies include producing movies and writing. He has produced three films that have been nominated for two regional Emmy® Awards. His movies support the message of foremost thought leaders with the likes of Rudy Ruettiger (inspiration for the Hollywood blockbuster *Rudy*), Brian Tracy (author of more than 70 books and world-famous trainer of 5,000,000 participants) and Jack Canfield (featured in the popular movie *The Secret*, and creator of the *Chicken Soup for the Soul* series).

His passion is supporting his clients' success in buying and selling their most valuable and sensitive asset—their home. Moreover, through his books, films and appearances, he aims to help people be successful in other areas of their lives as well.

He is the proud father of two sons, and spends his spare time with his lovely wife Vicki and their two cats, Teenie and Monkey.

To learn more about Johnny B visit: www.JohnnyB.com. For information about Johnny B's film projects go to: www.IMDb.me/JohnnyB or see the video of Johnny B being interviewed at Singularity University by the XGroup at: www.MeetJohnnyB.com.

Coldwell Banker
John Bretthauer Cal RE# 01480256

CHAPTER 3

THE IMPACT OF PRESTIGE: THE MORE POSITIVE THE PERCEPTION, THE BIGGER YOUR BUSINESS WINS

BY NICK NANTON & JW DICKS

The entrepreneur wanted to raise his profile.

He knew that the most successful people in their fields ended up being featured in traditional media outlets—such as cable news networks like *CNN* and *Fox*, newspapers like *The New York Times* and *The Washington Post*, and magazines like *Time* and *Newsweek*. These were media titans which were recognizable to everyone and appearing in any one of them brought you a huge elevation in prestige and respect in your industry. So, he began looking for a way to get his name in one of them.

He discovered a service where you could submit your name and your areas of expertise—and if that service accepted you, then you would end up on a list to receive emails from journalists looking for someone knowledgeable in a specific area. You could then respond with thoughts you could provide to the reporter, and, if the reporter saw value in those thoughts, they would write back.

And one day, one of those reporters did write back – and it was a reporter from *The New York Times*. Suddenly, the entrepreneur discovered to his delight, his name and some quotes from him were going to be featured in a prominent *Times* article.

Wow!

He suddenly felt his future was about to happen. Hey—he was about to become someone who was quoted in *The New York Times*! How cool was that? And how many phone calls and how much business would he receive as a result of this insanely great opportunity? He told his friends and family that the article would be published the next day—and to get ready for all the excitement that was about to happen.

The next day, everyone he had told about the article saw it in print or online and congratulated him. And then he waited for all those calls and all that new business to materialize.

. . . And he waited.

. . . And he waited.

Finally, a call came in from someone he didn't know who had seen his name in the article. And that person indeed wanted to talk business.

That person wanted to let the entrepreneur know that he could buy a plaque featuring a laminated version of the article to hang on his office wall. Wanting to get *something* out of the experience, he went ahead and bought that plaque—and did indeed hang it on his office wall.

Which turned out to be what *really* delivered the recognition he was after.

Prospects who came in to talk to him about a possible deal would always see the plaque on the wall. They would know he had been in *The New York Times* without him having to say a word about it. It impressed them and gave him more stature in their eyes.

And that's when it hit the entrepreneur. It wasn't about being in the media that makes you money. It was about how well you *marketed* the fact that you were in the media.

So, he put the fact that he appeared in the *New York Times* on his website. And in his bio. And suddenly, his credibility zoomed to new heights.

Nick Nanton had discovered a powerful way to not only raise his profile—but those of his clients as well.

Yes, this incident really happened to the co-author of this chapter. Early in his career, Nick, as any reasonable person might assume, thought appearing in *The New York Times* would automatically bring him some public recognition. However (and this is something we've both learned over the years), the impact of *any* media appearance, no matter how high-profile the outlet, quickly dissipates.

The upshot is this: Simply relying on making a media appearance to change your life is bound to leave you disappointed. However, *the value of prospects knowing about you being a part of a prestigious platform is incalculable.*

A true MediaMaster, our term for a thought leader who knows how to leverage both old and new media to build the most powerful platform possible, has to make their mark in arenas that are already perceived by the public as containing a high level of prestige. When you receive the "stamp of approval" from those kinds of platforms, your esteem rises sharply in the eyes of followers and prospects alike.

That's why, if you visit one of our websites, you're going to see a prominent section spotlighting our high-profile media appearances, with a title reading, "As Seen On..." and then a large collection of high-profile media names of where we have appeared. including not only *The New York Times*, but other recognizable names such as *USA Today, Newsweek, Forbes,* CBS, ABC, CNN, CNBC, *The Wall Street Journal*...well, the list goes on and on. Literally. At our CelebrityBrandingAgency. com site, you have to click on the bar to see the entire list of all the traditional media outlets we've been featured on.

Naturally, this collection of media can be very impressive if someone's checking us out on the web—after all, when you're considering whether to hire someone to raise your professional profile, it's a big advantage when you see that they've been in the mix with all those media giants. That's why we arrange for many of our clients to *also* be featured in these publications so they can use the same media names on most of *their* marketing materials. But it doesn't stop there. To add to their prestige factor, we host many events for our clients to speak at and participate in at high profile locations around the country each year. Additionally, we hold a red-carpet event for them in Hollywood at the Roosevelt Hotel, where the very first Academy Awards were held.

Adding this level of prestige to our clients' portfolios is one of our key marketing strategies to help them attain MediaMaster status. No one would disagree that you're guaranteed to create a massive impact when you can truthfully say you've been seen on CNN or in *BusinessWeek*—or that you were invited to speak at a major conference or venue—or that you were rocked in person by an amazing performance at a major televised awards ceremony. Suddenly, you've attained a certain stature that can't be denied or shrugged off. And you're on your way to being seen as much more than just "someone in the business," you start being seen as the *go-to expert*.

Prestige is the kind of intangible that automatically puts you in a different category than your competition. When you add it to your public perception, you increase your credibility, further your reach, and add incredible value to your profile.

The Prestige of Traditional Media

The main tactic to gain prestige that we're going to focus on in this chapter is by leveraging traditional media. This is one of our favorite ways to boost the prestige factor for our clients (and, to be honest, ourselves). Over the years, we've built a pretty bulletproof system to give our clients that big assist in prestige. We're going to talk about our specific methodology a little later. But first... let's talk a little about why traditional media does provide such a powerful impact for your persona. And we'll begin that conversation by digging in a little deeper on the differences between what we call *traditional media* and *new media*.

First, let's define our players in this match-up. When we talk about traditional media platforms, we're talking about the following:

- Print Publications (newspapers, magazines, journals, etc.)
- Radio stations and networks
- Television channels and networks

Now, all three of the above obviously have an additional online component these days, where they allow most of their content to be consumed, either through a subscription model, limited portions or even everything for free. But, in general, most traditional media outlets came into being long before anyone knew what an internet was and are still primarily perceived as offline entities.

In contrast, new media outlets only exist because of the introduction of the internet to the public. They include:

- Websites
- Blog sites
- Social media

- Online publications (such as Buzzfeed, Slate, Breitbart, Huffington Post, etc.
- Online video platforms (such as Vimeo, YouTube channels, and Facebook Live - even Amazon now has its own video content hub)

Although the actual content can be very similar on traditional and new media outlets, there are still several big and important differences between the two.

- **Traditional media is experienced more passively**

  Newspapers, TV and radio were designed to deliver entertainment and information to the public through what can only be seen as a one-way street. The most people could do to interact with these outlets would be to either call or write an actual letter to register a comment. With new media, the consumer has much more of a voice in the whole process. Sites like Netflix and Amazon feature content and promote products tailored to your past preferences, making new media more of a customized experience.

- **New media is more about engagement**

  Imagine someone watching an episode of, say, *The Brady Bunch*, in the 1970's and then being able to chat with people all over the world about what they liked and didn't like about the half-hour sitcom. You could only imagine it back then, because it simply wasn't possible.

  Today, it is. You can actually watch full episodes of the show on YouTube and immediately post an observation. Many entertainment sites post recaps of original shows that aired the night before and the debates over the show (as well as the recap) can go on for days in the comments section. Almost every online site encourages that kind of engagement and also includes links to their Twitter, Facebook and various other social media pages (just like our websites do). It's far from the one-way street of old media—it's more of a roundabout heading in all directions.

• **Traditional media is harder to penetrate**

As we mentioned, gatekeepers and their staff rule at traditional media. They have always used professional content producers, rarely featured outside work and have always had strict editorial standards in place for what they presented under their banner. It has always been very much a "closed" system that's difficult for newcomers to even have a shot at penetrating.

• **New media often features outside, "amateur" content under its umbrella**

"Aggregate" media sites, such as the Huffington Post, are famous (and sometimes infamous) for being largely composed of content gathered from other news sites (mostly traditional media ones!). Of course, much content is "borrowed" for social media pages and blog sites, just in order to create fresh posts on a regular basis, but this practice can't help but make new media seem a little less fresh and focused than traditional media. In addition, personal blogs and videos also often make their way onto these kinds of sites, making them seem more community-oriented and less based on the traditional system of professional journalists.

• **Traditional media is enhanced by its long history**

Even some of the youngest traditional media channels we've cited, such as CNN, are almost 40 years old. By contrast, the oldest new media channels are barely 21. That means the vast majority of the public grew up at a time when there was *only* traditional media—and that in turn means that that demographic can't help but have more respect for it.

- **New media is seen as less reliable (but this is rapidly changing)**

In the U.S. 2016 Presidential election, the term "fake news" became a household phrase, owing to the overflow of fabricated political reports aiming to take down specific candidates with false negative stories. Though there are some respected new media news and information sites, unfortunately, there are also an overabundance of legitimate-looking sites that do whatever they can to push a certain agenda or are simply "clickbait" (content whose main purpose is to attract attention and encourage visitors to click on a link to a particular web page). This growing practice negatively impacts all new media, creating a suspicious "Who can we trust?" atmosphere to internet content.

- **Traditional media is still the bedrock of trusted information**

Between new media and traditional media, which creates more respect and credibility for the MediaMaster? Well, there's really no contest. While new media may be the flashier, cooler new kid in town, traditional media channels still have a huge edge when it comes to the following crucial areas:

- Credibility
- Integrity
- Name Recognition
- Stability
- Stature

Yes, there is an argument to be made that the edge between New Media and Old Media is getting smaller every day. "Fake News" has become a factor in our lives. However, while there are certainly exceptions, content that isn't well-researched, thoroughly edited and fact-checked rarely survives the vetting process of traditional media. That's why traditional media still enjoys the level of prestige and trust that it does with most of the public. Granted, some may grant that prestige and trust to only *certain* traditional media outlets (there probably isn't much crossover between, say, MSNBC and FOX News audiences), but they do grant it.

This isn't to say you should abandon new media channels—far from it because, as we said, they are catching up every day. But when it comes to attaining the level of prestige that vaults you into a very select group, there are few methods more powerful than demonstrating a track record of traditional media exposure.

Traditional Media, Untraditional Methodology

Yes, traditional media can confer enormous prestige on those people who it spotlights. But it's also true that it can be incredibly difficult to get that spotlight on *you*. And that's precisely why we create our *own* quality content featuring our *own* clients, expressly designed to work with traditional media.

For example, we produce interview shows in studios all across the country, where our clients are interviewed by such MediaMaster legends as Jack Canfield and Brian Tracy. Here's a list of some of the shows we've made and the media outlets where they appeared:

- *Consumer's Advocate* – ABC, NBC, CBS, Fox
- *The Brian Tracy Show* – ABC, NBC, CBS, Fox
- *Hollywood Live with Jack Canfield* – Bravo, A&E
- *Success Today* – ABC, NBC, CBS, Fox
- *Get Real* – ABC, NBC, CBS, Fox
- *Times Square Today* – CNN, CNBC, Fox News
- *Wall Street Today* – CNN, CNBC, Fox News
- *Capitol Connection* – CNN, CNBC, Fox News

We produce these programs and place them on all kinds of traditional TV outlets, such as network affiliates and even the

Biography channel. And because we have the know-how to package these shows so they look as good (if not better) than other programming, the networks will take them and air them because our clients offer useful everyday advice in their area of expertise during their interviews. In other words, there is genuine *value* in the content we produce.

Same thing with print. We regularly produce magazine and newspaper features that profile our clients and showcase informative opinions and information that, again, the average reader can glean some value from. Some of those features have appeared under the headings of *"GameChangers," "Masters of Success"* and *"The Next Big Thing,"* where our clients predict a new huge trend coming to the business arena.

Through this professionally-produced content, many of our clients *will* find themselves on CNN. They *will* be featured in *USA Today* or any of the other numerous traditional media platforms we've already named in this chapter. And, again, ultimately, even though it's nice if someone actually sees that content, it's more important that our clients are able to add prestige to their portfolios by promoting these traditional media appearances.

Other Pillars of Prestige

Of course, there are other ways to build your prestige factor beyond leveraging traditional media. Let's break a few of them down by name and briefly discuss what they each bring to the table in terms of MediaMaster impact.

- **Awards**

  We recognize our clients who become Best-Selling Authors® by inducting them into the National Academy of Best-Selling Authors®, as well as by presenting them with our Quilly® Awards, designed to honor those whose books have been listed on any legitimate nationally-recognized Best-Seller list.

Whatever your field of expertise might be, there is almost a 100% chance that (a) there's a national or international organization built around that field and (b) that organization hosts some sort of award to recognize achievement in that field. Make an effort to win a few of those awards. When a large organization grants you official recognition of your expertise, it's another huge stamp of approval that will further your MediaMaster appeal if you market it correctly.

- **High-Profile Public Events**

When you show up at high-profile public events, whether it's a local community fair or a national big deal like the Grammys or Kentucky Derby, it demonstrates that you're comfortable in the limelight, you're connected to the right people and you're, as the credit card commercials used to say, "everywhere you want to be." Of course, the most important aspect of attending these events is making sure you use social media to publicize it—otherwise, most of your audience will never know you were there. Just be careful to make your posts funny, humble, appreciative... anything except self-aggrandizing.

- **Giving Back**

Don't get us wrong—we believe giving back isn't a tactic, it should be a part of everyone's daily lives. However, things like charitable donations, mentoring deserving young people and aligning yourself with a worthy cause do increase your prestige factor, because you're putting time, energy and/or money into an effort that helps the world at large, even if it's in a very small way. A MediaMaster should always have a pro-social component to their persona—it's a win-win for both you and the world. (See our book, *Mission-Driven Business*, for a whole lot more on this particular topic.)

- **Speaking Engagements**

  When you address large groups, you are automatically assigned a healthy boost of prestige. Not many people ever dare to venture into these waters, but a gifted speaker, particularly one seen in a visible and highly-regarded event or venue, is seen as a natural-born leader and definitely a MediaMaster. Whenever possible, have your speaking events put on video and post them on social media.

- **Celebrity Associations**

  Being associated in some way with a respected celebrity, a well-known personality, or a recognized leader in your field of expertise, is always impressive and delivers great impact. Look at the name on the cover of this book—Rudy Ruettiger, a guy who's been the subject of a big Hollywood movie and a documentary produced by the authors of this chapter. That name, and others like it, bring attention your way and also that all-important prestige factor.

- **Books and Movies**

  Authoring a book is an instant prestige generator, as well as having a branded movie made about you or your business. When a branded movie is professionally produced, it can create a very appealing and prestigious impact for any MediaMaster. Not only that, but there are more uses for a branded movie than you might realize. Besides placing it on social media and on your website, you can also have it played on local television stations either for free (if it spotlights a certain aspect of your community) or at low cost if you buy the time. We've also had clients rent out local movie theatres to premiere their branded films and that delivered sensational results for them.

In conclusion, to truly become a MediaMaster, you have to be seen as someone whose stature is greater than the norm. Prestige is the ticket to achieve that kind of stature and that prestige is generally granted by being seen in the right places (high-profile events, speaking events, etc.) and being recognized by established and respected entities (awards, traditional media, etc.). If you're an evolving MediaMaster, attaining that prestige will take you to a whole new level of success—and help you score the biggest "win" possible with your business!

About Nick

An Emmy Award-winning Director and Producer, Nick Nanton, Esq., produces media and branded content for top thought leaders and media personalities around the world. Recognized as a leading expert on branding and storytelling, Nick has authored more than two dozen Best-Selling books (including *The Wall Street Journal* Best-Seller, *StorySelling*™) and produced and directed more than 40 documentaries, earning 5 Emmy Awards and 14 nominations. Nick speaks to audiences internationally on the topics of branding, entertainment, media, business and storytelling at major universities and events.

As the CEO of DNA Media, Nick oversees a portfolio of companies including: The Dicks + Nanton Agency (an international agency with more than 3000 clients in 36 countries), Dicks + Nanton Productions, Ambitious.com, CelebrityPress, DNA Films®, DNA Pulse, and DNA Capital Ventures. Nick is an award-winning director, producer and songwriter who has worked on everything from large-scale events to television shows with the likes of Steve Forbes, Ivanka Trump, Sir Richard Branson, Rudy Ruettiger (inspiration for the Hollywood blockbuster, *RUDY*), Jack Canfield (*The Secret*, creator of the *Chicken Soup for the Soul* Series), Brian Tracy, Michael E.Gerber, Tom Hopkins, Dan Kennedy and many more.

Nick has been seen in *USA Today, The Wall Street Journal, Newsweek, BusinessWeek, Inc. Magazine, The New York Times, Entrepreneur® Magazine, Forbes,* and *FastCompany.* He has appeared on ABC, NBC, CBS, and FOX television affiliates across the country as well as on CNN, FOX News, CNBC, and MSNBC from coast to coast.

Nick is a member of the Florida Bar, a voting member of The National Academy of Recording Arts & Sciences (Home to the GRAMMYs), a member of The National Academy of Television Arts & Sciences (Home to the EMMYs), Co-founder of The National Academy of Best-Selling Authors®, and serves on the Innovation Board of the XPRIZE Foundation, a non-profit organization dedicated to bringing about "radical breakthroughs for the benefit of humanity" through incentivized competition – best known for its Ansari XPRIZE which incentivized the first private space flight and was the catalyst for Richard Branson's Virgin Galactic.

Nick also enjoys serving as an Elder at Orangewood Church, working with Young Life, Downtown Credo Orlando, Entrepreneurs International and rooting for the Florida Gators with his wife Kristina and their three children, Brock, Bowen and Addison.

Learn more at:
- www.NickNanton.com
- www.CelebrityBrandingAgency.com

About JW

JW Dicks, Esq., is a *Wall Street Journal* Best-Selling Author®, Emmy Award-Winning Producer, publisher, board member, and co-founder of organizations such as The National Academy of Best-Selling Authors®, and The National Association of Experts, Writers and Speakers®.

JW is the CEO of DNAgency and is a strategic business development consultant to both domestic and international clients. He has been quoted on business and financial topics in national media such as *USA Today, The Wall Street Journal, Newsweek, Forbes, CNBC.com*, and *Fortune Magazine Small Business*.

Considered a thought leader and curator of information, JW has more than forty-three published business and legal books to his credit and has co-authored with legends like Jack Canfield, Brian Tracy, Tom Hopkins, Dr. Nido Qubein, Dr. Ivan Misner, Dan Kennedy, and Mari Smith. He is the Editor and Publisher of *ThoughtLeader®* Magazine.

JW is called the "Expert to the Experts" and has appeared on business television shows airing on ABC, NBC, CBS, and FOX affiliates around the country and co-produces and syndicates a line of franchised business television shows such as *Success Today, Wall Street Today, Hollywood Live*, and *Profiles of Success*. He has received an Emmy® Award as Executive Producer of the film, *Mi Casa Hogar*.

JW and his wife of forty-three years, Linda, have two daughters, three granddaughters, and two Yorkies. He is a sixth-generation Floridian and splits his time between his home in Orlando and his beach house on Florida's west coast.

CHAPTER 4

MY CALLING

BY AUDREY KIMNER

As I sit next to the fire at Pebble Beach Lodge, I reflect on what it truly means to win in life. Only close friends and family know that my life has been lived in reverse. As a teenager, a client suggest I work in her building, the Pennzoil building in downtown Houston. The clientele consisted of oil and gas executives, bankers, lawyers, judges and brokers. The economy was booming in the eighties and I was only eighteen years old.

Every morning in the underground tunnel, life was not uncommon to see executives having their shoes shined while drinking vodka. This big, wide open stage lasted over a span of ten years and I had no idea how this time would set up my entire life going forward. The brilliant clientele taught me how to network, invest, where to travel and all with exquisite manners.

I was raised in a loving home with an adventurous family. My father, a US Navy Master Chief, joined NASA in Houston as an engineer. My brother, father and grandfather all served our country and sheriff's department. My mother was in sales of hardwood floors and steel while my family were all successful small business owners.

My grandfather was a visionary and a cattleman, owning ranches in Oklahoma and Texas. My grandfather always shared stories with us about owning our own businesses and how to manage people for success. Although a simple man, he was very wise and his stories still remain with me. He loved his family and lived life to the fullest. In fact, both my grandparents enjoyed having their pilot licenses. We all raced boats, sailed, hunted, fished, danced and enjoyed our communities. My family has allowed me to venture into anything where I chose to win.

In my twenties, I joined the Urban Retreat of Houston. The president, Francie Willis was a hard act to follow as she was voted top business women in the *Wall Street Journal.* After traveling and promoting her businesses globally, I see how working with the best and observing is a win.

In 1997, I married an oil and gas Duke Energy executive, and two years later we had two children, Cameron and Jordan. We both climbed the ladder of success and retired in our early thirties. Interior design was my passion, so I started collecting art and antiques along our travels. I worked with architects on our homes from start to the finishing touches in décor. All of the builders would offer me jobs, but working from home allowed me to volunteer, study and raise my children. Winning to me is learning how to balance family and your passions while continuing to thrive by learning something new daily.

During my years of working, I continued the path of thriving in subjects like business and design. The life of creating in color, design, painting and drawing will open one's eye and soul like no other. Winning to me is walking out of the door and noticing the shapes of the clouds, the color of the sky, the shape of every object and palate of my surroundings, including beautiful fabrics and rugs. All of my interests lead me down the road of history of antiques, rugs and the world of travel. Winning to me is learning the culture that surrounds us between objects and people across the world.

As an athlete growing up, my drive for competition was lacking. Golf seemed to be the only sport that I was never introduced too, so I took golf lessons. Little did I know, golf is an addiction like no other. My love of golf turned into my social life and time with my children while teaching them etiquette, manners and a different type of history. Golf took us to courses all over the US while spending quality time together. We all played on golf teams and caddied for each other. We laughed along the way with silly golf shots and making a few holes-in-one. Golf was a win for us and the memories are priceless.

As our children went to school full time and the Enron bust was the talk of the country, life took a huge shift. My vibrant rock of a spouse was making bad decisions and acting out in front of us. He started binge drinking, doing illegal drugs and became very controlling and abusive. In 2008, my ex-husband took his aggression out on myself and our children. After trying to de-escalate the situation and leave with my children, I had to call the police. The arrest took place and our world was never the same. I helped tremendously, but later it was clear his intentions were to move money, set me up legally and retaliate. I filed for divorce in 2010.

Not being able to exit at a moment's notice, I was followed around our home with a camera in the back of my head by him trying to make me react. He shut off my credit cards while he used our children as a weapon against me. My life became a horror movie in my own home. While my lawyer, Alex Cash, Esq. refused to protect me, stand up for me or stop the financial abuse, he used us three to intentionally drain my accounts. My children were forced to live in danger and unprotected by the law.

My lifestyle was also a weapon to discriminate and bully me by my own counsel team, Robert Rosen, Alex Varner and Alex Cash. I hired Earle Lilly after not getting help from South Carolina attorneys. One would think the best interest of my children would come first, along with a fiduciary duty to me, but this was not the case. I discovered my computer was wiretapped and my attorney-privileged emails were sent to Lori Stoney, Esq. and Paul Tinkler, Esq. A key-logger and g-mail gadget were attached to my email, which is a federal and state offense. Also, attorneys became accessories to a crime. I find it hard to describe the invasion of my privacy. I was horrified by the entire state's failure to protect us as a domestic violence victim. My children were later extorted for my assets while I was detained on a flight due to a passenger having a heart attack and I was never served a change of custody. It has been over two and a half years without contact with my children as Jerry Theos, Lori Stoney, Margaret Theos and Suzanne Groff have tried to unsuccessfully throw out my appeal. I will write a book about my experience during wiretapping and endangerment to my children.

After severe misrepresentation, I quickly realized this legal battle was my own. Having never been to law school, I learned the laws. I encompassed every piece of knowledge and evidence to court with me. I learned the objections and procedures of the court as a pro se litigant.

The fuel that fired my soul to seek justice came after I won twice in court. A judge was forced to call a mistrial due to the evidence I placed on the record. The explosion came when I made all accountable on the record and filed a lawsuit.

As my title "mom" first, the battle was on. I took off for months to review emails and wrote the lawyer conduct and judicial boards. I took my proof to the Charleston Police Department solicitor and interviewed civil attorneys. I made a decision to represent myself after being bullied by the courts and police, along with excuses from attorneys. I used my proof to set the entire family court community up for a superb civil case. I made all tainted emails public record by copying the police, which refused to file charges and protect us. I told the truth on my Facebook page for my safety and for all judges to read the truth. Later, Lori Stoney admitted to abusing the courts for revenge of his domestic violence arrest.

Since I documented myself being wiretapped and used the law, I backed every SC attorney, judge and court clerk back into a corner with their own legal game and a paper trail that nobody could deny.

I started to feel empowered by learning federal and state laws. The wealth of knowledge combined with the love for my children made me unstoppable. I connected with other litigants in all fifty states and began posting the constitutional rights, along with the invaluable knowledge I learned from interviewing bar members, which were fearful. Their fear renewed my soul, faith and dedication to all children.

My inquisitive mind lead an unexpected path and forced me to think outside the box. As I head to the Supreme Court next month, I know there are no winners in family court, only a desperate need to reform a broken system which destroys the family fabric, mental health of children and causes irreversible harm. I will forever advocate for children and those with no voice.

I encourage the law to be taught in all schools going forward, along with new ways of learning from the documentary, *Most Likely To Succeed.* I want to thank all whom have become my extended family and worked to implement laws. Many new author friends are here to stay due to family court, especially Jodi Parmley and Janet Delfuoco. I want to thank Jodi Mueller for making parental alienation an awareness day, and Jeff Morgan for lobbying grandparent rights in TX and taping videos of victims of domestic violence by proxy. This new term is being used for litigants abusing the courts via third parties. Prayers to all that are affected by Title IV-D of The Social Security Act and the alienation of their own children, especially Julie Goffstein who has not seen her boys in years due to her Jewish religion. I also want to thank Kash Jackson for his efforts to bring awareness, especially for our military. Most of all I want to thank my family for never leaving my side.

Little did I know adversity would be my number one teacher. As in golf, I don't lay up nor do I quit. After years of single parenting, I had to dig down deep and ask myself, what are my passions? What sets my soul on fire every day? What makes me jump out of bed and ready to start my day and end at midnight with excitement? What can I pass down to my children as my legacy? My answers were golf and design while traveling the world. Hanging in a bar with people half my age was not winning, so I started to research group travel for golf.

I do believe what you think about happens, good or bad. In golf, we call it the mental game. The pros at my golf club were going to Scotland and the British Open. This was fitting for my plan on my personal time. I was grateful to be invited by two personal friends and PGA coaches. I quickly learned the twenty people attending were friends in the golf world. I cannot explain the spiritual trip that Scotland turned out to be. The new friends and caddies were spectacular and the gold coast scenery was fabulous.

On the last round of our trip, it was pouring down rain. We were determined to play what I call Scottish golf. Our pro caddies placed umbrellas over our clubs and were first class. As I rounded the turn at the Castle Course, I put dry towels in my bag. At the next hole, I realized nothing was dry inside my golf bag. I thought to myself, why don't they make these bags waterproof? We have water resistant fabrics readily available, so my mind started turning. As most women know, golf accessories, especially bags for women, are a void in the market. Also, a beautiful and functional golf bag is, and has been, nonexistent in my fifteen years of playing recreationally and competitively. I flew home and started designing my own bag. My bag has opened life to travel, especially due to the fact of not having factories in the USA.

The marketing of my bag has taken me all over the world and social media. I was also contacted to share a spot on the Brian Tracy Show. As in golf, I go for every shot! I do not lay up and

I never lay down in life. I don't believe in failure or the word failure. In my opinion, we learn from life and every adventure we choose, even the bad, is part of our journey. Winning is making the calls, telling your story and researching the industry in every aspect. The numbers will surprise you as only twenty percent of women play golf. I want to grow the game and most women are drawn to beautiful things such as fashion and feminine accessories.

Not only is my bag for women, because I am approached by men wanting a functional bag as well. As the golf industry grows, we should all keep in mind the collaboration of golf and tech. Stay tuned to what my bags have to offer with the new tech gadgets to improve all golf games.

I will offer golf tips that helped me learn the game quickly and I would suggest hiring a PGA pro to learn the basic swing. I watched professional golf, videos and the golf channel often. I played golf with men to up my game as much as possible. I would suggest practicing and to touch a club daily while putting for fun with your spouse and children. I read about golf and it wasn't until I read Zen Golf that my handicap dropped to scratch. I want to share that relaxing and enjoying the day is the best for success in golf.

My golf bag business has become my new challenge and mental game of a win. I am thriving and leaving my legacy for my children. I have named the Camjor golf bag after my two children, Cameron and Jordan. As Rudy and I have experienced, dream and dream again.

About Audrey

Audrey Kimner is an Interior Designer, golf bag designer and scratch golfer. She grew up in Houston, Texas and moved to Charleston, South Carolina to raise her children. Audrey relocated to Pebble Beach, California after traveling and designing her own innovative golf bag.

After interviewing with Brian Tracy in California concerning her golf bag, she flew to Pebble Beach to play the courses and research fabrics to make a prototype. She stayed at the Pebble Beach Lodge for a few weeks and fell in love with the area. She chose to stay to write several books, and thought this would be a perfect place to enjoy the scenery while spending time in the surrounding areas for business purposes.

The mornings and evenings around the Lodge were so uplifting. She would enjoy writing overlooking the water and meeting so many incredible people. The top-notch employees were so gracious and shared in her excitement of the golf bag idea, golf and books. The locals introduced her to everyone to seal the deal for the final technology ideas requested for her bag, and she also began volunteering for the AIM Foundation. The beaches, art, wine tasting, local fresh markets, golf, whale watching and fantastic people all lured her to stay.

AIM, mental health research for children, is so important and she had negative experiences concerning her own children in the South Carolina family courts. She believes the mental health for all would be relieved with new laws, awareness and education involving the court communities and the public. Children rarely have a voice and are not taught to be innovative. She recently viewed a documentary called *Most Likely to Succeed* on this subject with her friend and future co-author, Tracy A. LeBlanc.

As she shares Rudy's vision, she is amazed at the parallels in their lives. Having gone through a similar experience, she knows having a dream should always be backed up with something to look forward to. She feels she is a true survivor of domestic violence and our biased legal system, but remains confident that the best is yet to come. Winning is not what happens to you, but how you learn from your experience and use it for your own divine purpose.

CHAPTER 5

THE "MAGIC" THAT HELPS YOU *WIN* AND KEEP WINNING

BY BROCK MEADOWS

We all want to WIN. Of course we do. And there is no shortage of success stories and those that achieved it that tell us how they did it. However, that seldom provides a precise roadmap to simply insert oneself and follow the "yellow-brick" road to arrive at OZ.

Each and every journey is unique. In fact, if there was a 'do over' for their big success, it most likely would not occur in the exact same way it did the first time. There's far too many factors beyond one's control, and trying to plot the exact steps is next to impossible. That's not to say it's not positive, or worth something. On the contrary, that makes the story even more fascinating.

Look at the differences in wins and losses in sports. Two teams can have the same playbook, strategy, philosophy, and even ability, but the preparation, practice, timing and execution will be completely different. Furthermore, when you consider the intangibles of heart, loyalty, hunger and attitude, you and I both know the difference in results can be like night and day.

Mohammed Ali said that he was not made a champion in the ring, but was only recognized as one there. It was all the hard work, sacrifice and dedication that he put towards his quest, when it wasn't visible to the public, that made him the champion we all saw him as.

So, rather than study a person's success in an effort to duplicate it, choose to study the person—their individual characteristics and traits. There you find items like: belief, faith, purpose, drive, discipline, commitment, desire and work ethic. You learn that no matter how great one's ability or drive is, there is seldom any shortcut on the path to success. You must show up everyday, put in the work, commit to the process, lean into the pain and inch yourself forward.

You also begin to understand the process they encountered and to learn the decisions made along the journey that created the development for their achievement. When you do that, you find the real reasons, often unnoticed, for the success everyone now sees. The "magic" that helped them WIN and KEEP WINNING is discovered in the journey, not the destination.

This approach proves to be incredibly encouraging for it will reveal two critical truths for winning in virtually every facet of life:

1. You don't have to have the complete roadmap to begin your journey – you just need to have the Faith and Desire to start.

2. There is a process of development that is associated with every achievement.

I was 22 years old, had just completed an amazing experience of a lifetime in association with the '96 Olympics in Atlanta, GA and graduated from Bowling Green State University in Ohio.

I was offered a pretty awesome job as the Director of Marketing for a large company in downtown Atlanta. After 14 months of working there, I came to the conclusion that corporate America and the typical environment associated with it was not for me. I clearly remember having the burning thought that if I didn't do something about it now, I'd be 40 and "stuck" somewhere I knew I would not be happy.

I vividly recall the moment I entered the President's office to submit my resignation. I was nervous, and a little scared too. I didn't want to disappoint him, my family or my future, but I just knew this wasn't where I was supposed to be. When Mr. Williams asked, "So what are you going to do?" The very first thing that came to my mind was, "I'm going to coach. I'm not exactly sure in what capacity, but whatever I do, it will include coaching people to help them become more."

That may sound like a line I was trying to give to him to just get out of there, but it was the honest-to-goodness truth. I even surprised myself when I heard the words come out of my mouth. I guess you could say it was my moment of enlightenment.

Mr. Williams was great, but I could tell he was looking for something more concrete from me. So, after a few minutes of trying to convince me to give it some more time and thought, I kindly, and still with a little fear in my gut, said, "Thank you so much for the opportunity. I don't exactly know what my path is, but I do know this place and position is not where I'm suppose to be to accomplish it."

Looking back on that pivotal moment, I was blessed to be compelled with the strong feelings that: *the first step towards getting somewhere is to decide you are not going to stay where you are.* I had seen other people compromise and settle for the "safer" path, only to be unfulfilled and unhappy. When you keep going with the flow and taking the path of least resistance, you'll not only greatly underperform your talent, but you'll live a life that will always leave you wondering – "What if?" And fortunately for me, staying there was a far greater discomfort than stepping out on faith that there was more for me elsewhere.

That is when I discovered the strength and peace of knowing what you *DON'T* want.

Knowing what you don't want can guide and drive you more than knowing what you do want.

Stay with me on this for a moment, this is a winning perspective that hasn't gotten the attention it deserves.

For example, never wanting to not have the freedom to be with my family if there was a crisis or significant need. During my first six months on that job, my father had a heart attack and quadruple bypass surgery. He was single and I needed to be with him to help. I was only gone for two days when I received a call from the office that I was needed, and was expected to be back by the end of the week. I was furious and frustrated. I couldn't believe it. This was new to me, but I quickly came to learn that's just the way it was in the "normal" corporate world.

From that point on, I started to change my thinking and become more aware of what I didn't want to have to tolerate in my life, and what I would have to start doing in order to make that happen. Settling was certainly not going to be my story.

Knowing what you don't want also helps you accept not having to have all the answers in order to start, and to avoid being paralyzed to make a decision. And while I didn't have a roadmap for what was next, I gained confidence by having clarity for the things I didn't want. Thank goodness that was enough to cause me to make a decision and move.

Now this may surprise you, but the next step I took wasn't where I experienced my "success," nor did it fit into the answer I gave

Mr. Williams for what I was going to do next. But it was exactly where I was supposed to be in that time in my life to ultimately help me become more. This is the important part of the "process" I referred to earlier, and I think a lot of times is marginalized or undervalued.

Why? Because it's usually not a lot of fun when you are going through it. It's tough, never sexy, and certainly not instant. To fully gain from it, rarely can short cuts be taken. That definitely does not stop people from trying though, and that's where we find a lot of people in today's internet, social media-driven marketplace, promoting themselves as an expert without much experience to support their claim.

They often attempt to model someone else's success, not having gone through the process of development for themselves, or even studied that part of the person's success they are trying to emulate, and are left disappointed and frustrated, wondering why it's not working for them.

I truly believe in order to accomplish high-level success and consistently win in your efforts, one must have the knowledge that it is far more about the person you become in pursuit of the things you want. Growth precedes achievement.

It was my first crack at entrepreneurship, and the place me and my partner selected to do it was the furthest we could go, while still being in a U.S. territory – St. Thomas, U.S.V.I.

Now isn't it interesting that nearly every great success we hear about, often found them living in less than desirable spaces when they were first getting started and making their way? Some in a shelter, or living in garage of a buddy's home, or in a make-shift apartment in a marina that had them sleeping on a plywood floor. Well, the latter example was my situation. Only I had an air mattress my mom sent me that unfortunately received a hole in it quickly that only allowed it to hold air for a couple hours before I was awakened and had to refill it.

This adventure was the most challenging and difficult of my young life. Very few things, if any, went as we had planned for. In many ways, I can best describe it as an absolute butt-whooping. But I was consistently fueled by three things:
- knowing what I didn't want
- making sure I never settled
- living true to who I believe I was called to be

That was the gift of this season of life. As wild and unpredictable as it was, I came to discover more about myself, my weaknesses and strengths, my passion and dreams, my likes and dislikes, my values and goals. I learned so much about people, relationships, business, health, and spirituality. It was an intense crash course in self-discovery and business training that everyone should go through, but so few do.

By getting away from the comfort and conveniences of what I was accustomed to, I was better able to identify and appreciate what I truly wanted, by defining what I didn't want. That is a principle that every person that wants to win must not overlook. Because, *most people do not truly cut through the noise of the outside world to look within themselves to learn why they do what they do or don't do, what they truly want and what they don't want.*

The great majority of people can rattle off the things they think they want in life. Things that will make life better and happier. That's easy and fun. The problem with that is those are things they have little attachment to because they have not yet experienced them. The feeling and emotion is not as strong as something you have actually experienced.

Don't misunderstand, dreams are wonderful, and fun to have for the hope of things to come. But, because our "wants" are positioned in the future, we often put off the actions required to move towards them for another day – hence the common saying, "I'll start tomorrow."

For example, say you set out to lose 20 lbs. and get in amazing shape to look your best ever on the beach. You want to have no shame in your game and feel incredibly confident in your skin. Over a few weeks you have lost 10 pounds. You are feeling good and excited about your results. You go to a summer cookout and you're met with several enticing dishes that will sabotage your progress. If you're only motivated by what you want, the idea itself, but have never been and felt amazing in your swimsuit (since your early twenties), most likely you talk yourself into thinking, what's one or two desserts going to do? I've lost 10 lbs. and have done great. I deserve it.

On the other hand, what if you clearly identified the things you DON'T want? Things you are unwilling to continue tolerating? Recalling the very consequences that caused you PAIN. "Last year at the beach, I stayed covered up and didn't get to fully enjoy a vacation. I've lost 10 pounds and there is no way I'm letting myself lose ground and head back to a weight that negatively affected my life and happiness." Because the pain is REAL, you start to become uncomfortable. You know exactly how that makes you feel. There's no guessing or wondering. You lived it. And for that reason, you know without a doubt, you don't want to feel that way again. So you display mental strength and self-discipline and confidently walk away and don't give it another thought.

This not only applies to your health and fitness, but just about everything in life:
- Not making the team or riding the bench.
- Not being able to afford a family vacation.
- Being unsure if you can pay all your business bills this month.
- Losing in any fashion.

I'm confident you'd find putting things off, and doing the things you know you should do, but don't want to, become less and less frequent. You begin to discover the healthy push for the avoidance of pain.

... That makes for a strong attribute to hold yourself accountable.

You be the judge. Here's a simple, but not easy working exercise for you to complete. Before you read further and begin the exercise, answer this question: What do you say causes you to get into Action and stay consistent in those actions to accomplish success?

> a) The Desire for Gain?
> b) The Avoidance of Pain?

Now take out a piece of paper. Draw a vertical line down the center. Label the left side: Things I Don't Want, and the right side: Things I Do Want. (Basically, "Pain" and "Gain.")

Give serious, concentrated thought to each side individually for as long as you need to elicit emotion and get to what truly matters. Once completed, and starting on the left side of the page, read each item on your list out loud. Next, read your list on the right. Which side of the page hits you most? Stirs you up a bit? Makes you a little uncomfortable and gets you fired up?

They're both valuable, but what I know is this: Goals and Dreams are targets and desired outcomes that give us something to aim for. Knowing what you want absolutely helps set a destination.

Pain and Intolerance is the fuel and drive to keep showing up consistently to move ourselves forward to accomplish the things we want. ***Knowing what you don't want provides the fuel needed to create the changes and take the actions necessary to make what you do want a reality.***

What I believe you'll begin to see is the items you listed on the left will in fact be the very reasons you will achieve the items on the right.

The avoidance of pain is a critical driver that encourages discomfort, helps you stay hungry and "in the game." That's valuable fuel when we know success is a comfort only awarded to those that are willing to do the uncomfortable – a most positive place to be for that's where Growth best occurs. And we all can agree that:

> *Without growth, there is little to no success.*

Don't spare the rod and don't allow the fear of the finish to belittle your faith to start.

> *Embrace the process and enjoy the journey. That's how you go for the win.*

About Brock

Brock Meadows is a fitness and nutrition professional with nearly 20 years of experience and an extensive background as an NSCA - Certified Strength and Conditioning Specialist that has coached thousands of men and women across the country, including elite and professional athletes.

In 2001, he started his own performance training program. With creative use of resources and space, on a minimal budget, he began training athletes and local sports teams. From there he expanded his business into his own facility in Marion, Ohio (Power Factory) for athletes and the general population. With 5,000 square feet, 25 yards of turf, two other trainers, and a partnership with a local hospital providing physical therapy on site, he began pursuing his dreams of business ownership and making a difference in the very community where he grew up.

His training and expertise has grown the past 10 years to include nutrition coaching with both training and non-training clients throughout the country. His perspective that people can choose not to workout and exercise daily, but they will eat something every day, prompted Brock to build a solution for the biggest piece of the overall health and wellness puzzle – nutrition. This different approach and unique program increased results for training clients, naturally fueled referrals inside and outside Power Factory, and ultimately revealed the amazing ability to expand his reach beyond four walls. Through a specific curriculum, personal coaching and active engagement in a supportive environment, his nutrition business experienced massive growth.

As a result, he began teaching and training other fitness pros on how to do the same. He did this by leveraging their knowledge and expertise, and multiplying their impact and income. In July of 2015, he sold Power Factory to focus on the continued growth of his nutrition and coaching business, and be a work from home husband to his wife, Nicole, and father to their two boys, Camden and Brexden.

Today, in addition to his F.I.T. Nutrition Coaching platform, Brock is an investor, owner of two Orangetheory Fitness franchises, and works with companies and individuals to increase team and personal performance. His passion is helping clients discover winning strategies that fit them personally – taking them from where they are to where they want to be.

To view more about the F.I.T. Nutrition Coaching program, visit:
- YourFitJourney.com

Or connect with Brock at:

- FB: @brockmeadowscoaching
- LinkedIn
- InstaGram: @brockjm4
- Twitter: @brockmeadows

CHAPTER 6

AT THE TABLE WITH RUDY

BY JARED ANDERSON PINO

To be frank, I had never actually seen the iconic film prior to deciding to attend the University of Notre Dame. The movie *Rudy* was familiar to me solely as a classic film that I had been told was worth watching—something that parallels *The Longest Yard, Hoosiers*, and *Chariots of Fire*. It honestly was nothing more. I had heard of it but I had never seen it first-hand. In fact, my affiliation with the university had for the longest time not extended beyond the fact that my dad had gone there as an undergrad from '69 to '73. Luckily, that did not dissuade me from applying—and rather encouraged me—whereas the adverse effect occurred with my brother, Jordan, who preferred the urban Jesuit Boston College to the Holy Cross Fathers of rural South Bend.

Unlike many of the students on campus today, I was not a diehard Domer who lived and breathed ND gold and blue. Embarrassingly enough, Lou Holtz was just a name. And, it would take me from the time I was accepted several days prior to April 1, 2016, the deadline for college responses, all the way until early August when I began planning and preparing for move-in weekend, to truly adopt that sense of quasi-patriotism and loyalty towards my future alma mater.

So, when I first watched *Rudy* at a friend's house early on in the summer after I had graduated from Lake Highland Prep, it was nothing more than a whim. Having said that, however, it was at that moment—when the credits began to run across the TV screen—that I understood the power of *Rudy* that had been described to me for so many years. The perseverance and resilience of the character Rudy was powerful and effectual, and the cinematography incredible. I believe the movie, coupled with other events, was the perfect set-up for my first semester at Notre Dame.

Fast-forwarding to the Spring of 2017, I was in the second semester of my freshman year and enjoying every minute of it—excluding the hard work, of course. I received an email from my godfather, Jack W. Dicks, explaining to me the ideas behind and the intended purposes of this project. In that email, he also invited me to meet the real "Rudy" Ruettiger and hear his story while they shot video and conducted several interviews on campus and throughout South Bend. I was shocked to say the least, while simultaneously feeling honored and humbled. After all, I was a freshman at the time without any relationship to any important figure; at least, so I thought. Little did I know, however, that "Uncle Jack" (who we called my godfather), and his partner and the movie director, Nick Nanton, were in charge of bringing Rudy's true story to an entirely new generation and audience of admirers.

As you probably know, whether it be the newest generation or past ones, the original movie received vast admiration for its brilliant quality. Yet, the movie did not pass without criticism. Some took issue with the original movie citing evidence of inaccuracies and/or exaggerations in certain parts. For example—and I could cite several—Rudy is put in the game against Georgia Tech in the final moments of the film, but a Boston College banner is in the stands, since the shot was filmed during a 1992 BC game, not a Georgia Tech game. And so forth and so on.

But inaccuracies of movie-making aside, one particular observation kept coming up for me. A movie is a movie; it is not a biography. It is intrinsically geared towards entertainment, regardless of how true the producers and writers intend to keep the story. Chances are very strong that mistakes will happen, and they do! So, with that in mind, some truths can, and often do, get morphed and under- or over-exaggerated. But does that matter? Should I care, for example, whether certain characters were or were not based on specific named individuals? In the case of Rudy, the controversy was perhaps over-hyped. Some characters, such as the groundskeeper and Rudy's older brother, Frank, were actually composite characters who represented the many who encouraged, and some who discouraged, Rudy, respectively. But is that such a bad thing? Is that nothing other than simple creative liberty? Is not the creative license irrelevant to the story line anyway?

Robert Kiyosaki and his book, *Rich Dad, Poor Dad*, for example, took similar heat. Unbeknownst to most people, Robert Kiyosaki did not have a "rich dad," nor did he have a "poor dad." He had countless people in his life as he grew up who together represented both his rich dad—who lived from a position of abundance and prosperity—and his poor dad—who lived from a position of scarcity. He wrote the story to represent the points of view of all those he characterized. While that might have generated controversy when first discovered, which it did, that controversy dissipated after Kiyosaki described the differences between the two of them as well as the impact those characters had on his life's development, which is really the point anyway. So too was the story about Rudy. He ran the gauntlet between those who encouraged and discouraged him, individuals reflected compositely. To me, the movie had nothing to do with that issue though—*Rudy* is about inspiration. It is about resilience. And above all, it is about redemption.

I descended the stairs of Tippecanoe Restaurant to the lower level looking for Uncle Jack. The walls were covered with South

Bend and Studebaker paraphernalia. As I learned later that night, the restaurant originally belonged to the Studebaker family in the late 1800's. It now serves as a lavish restaurant with fine dining. In this case, it served as the base-of-operations for the film crew while they were in South Bend.

My first introduction to Rudy came shortly after coming downstairs. It was the first time I had met a famous person, and I was pleasantly surprised (the second time occurred in September during the Georgia game when I snapped a photo with Speaker of the House, Paul Ryan). After some photos and light talk, we made our way over for dinner. At dinner, I listened to story after story and memory after memory. "Is the bar called 'Corby's' still around?" Rudy asked the table. "Yes," I answered. Rudy commented on his time speaking with current ND students from earlier that day. He reflected on how heart-warming it was to see the faces of some students light up when they realized it was *the* Rudy with whom they were speaking.

I could go on and on and give voice to the chit-chat among us sitting across the table from Rudy, but, at the end of the day, here are just a few observations I had while at the table with Rudy that night that I would like to share with you.

OBSERVATION #1

Sausage making ain't pretty. Life is not nearly as clean or pristine as we would like it to be. Rudy is not a guy who necessarily had a clean life. The stories he told, and the way in which he told them, indicated that life had not always been so straightforward, or spotless, or perfect for him as he might have preferred. But he did not let that stop him. As every student seeks to not let a poor grade or tough class discourage him or her, it is also crucial to always remind ourselves to brush it off, get back up, and get on with it. I see it with some of my friends and classmates a year or two ahead of me in the rigorous process of applying and interviewing for business internships and jobs. As

72

I'm sure most of those reading know far more than I, it's a dim and disheartening process. But most of those who are successful go through that process. Rudy did. He, quite literally, took each sack, got back up on his feet, and went at it again. And even off the field, after graduation, he continued to do so, packing his sausages with whatever was available, edible or not.

OBSERVATION #2

As lyricized by the great Nina Simone and modernized by Kanye West, JAY-Z, and J. Cole, in life, *we gotta do what we gotta do.* I happen to live in Orlando, Florida, home of Disney World, in which characters come and go. But, at the end of the day, every Disney movie always has a happy Disney ending. Life does not work that way. In life, people have to do uncomfortable and, sometimes questionable, things... for those they love and sometimes to just make things happen. Rudy might not always have been proud of what he did, but he did what he had to do, when he had to do it. Life, as we all know, doesn't work that way.

OBSERVATION #3

Kicking and screaming aren't child's play. The Longest Yard positions selflessness, sacrifice, and perseverance to band together individuals into a team driven to succeed at their mission. Irrespective of how Rudy's life unfolded—sometimes making sausage, oftentimes doing what he had to do, and occasionally kicking and screaming along the way—he was currently walking the Notre Dame campus with a film production company making a movie about himself. Impressive. A documentary and a book are being made about Rudy. Rudy persevered and he succeeded and now, here he is.

OBSERVATION #4

It's not about how you begin. In some cases, it is not even about how you make the sausages. Many times, it is about how you end it, how you finish. Said from a different perspective, you might be kicked in the beginning. You might be kicked throughout the whole duration of the process. But at the end, where do you intend to be? For Rudy, like Eric and Hariot in *Chariots of Fire*, it's crossing the finish line earning a gold medal.

OBSERVATION #5

Life teaches you how to live it. I accept that I know very little. This may come as a surprise to my parents. My dad would tell me stories about how, during college, he thought he knew everything and his parents—my grandparents—knew nothing. But he also said that it would take him into his mid-20s to realize how very little he actually knew. After experiencing the real world, he realized two things: first, he knew close to nothing; and second, he need not be worried, because it was part of the process. Life teaches you how to live it. It taught my dad, it taught Rudy. It will teach me. Nobody could have encapsulated it better than Tony Bennett at the end of the Amy biopic on Amy Winehouse, where he paid tribute to Amy, commenting sadly that life really is a pretty good teacher if you just give it the chance to teach. Rudy gave life that chance and he is showing us all what that can mean.

As I walked away from the table and from Rudy, and before I ascended the stairs to exit the original Studebaker mansion, I looked back over my shoulder one last time and saw his face, realizing where he had come from, and where he was going. I felt in my bones, as fleeting as that might otherwise be, that Rudy's indefatigable spirit had become the life he lived: it parlayed him onto the Notre Dame football field as an improbable walk-on years ago, immortalized in the iconic movie that became a precursor for the life he in fact lived, and gave him the opportunity to learn the lessons life had provided—lessons that each one of us someday will be able to self-assess, embrace, and possibly apply.

But, most importantly, from the perspective of a sophomore at the University of Notre Dame, who has not collected all that much personal life experience to support my observations and life lessons, I think every reader who opens up this book will bring to bear an intuitive understanding of a major takeaway that deserves highlighting. For Rudy, as well as for each of us, nothing is more real, more valued, or more central than seeing our lives—battered, bruised, and scarred—as a landscape for the redemption we all seek in continuing to correct our pasts and doing better in our futures. We strive, like Rudy, to be the person he hoped and still hopes to be, as he (years ago and over the past several days) strolled the Notre Dame campus under the sunlit Golden Dome.

About Jared

Jared Pino currently attends the University of Notre Dame. He is in his second year, studying finance and political science. Jared was born and raised in Winter Park, Florida, a city just outside of Orlando, Florida. Prior to attending university, he went to Lake Highland Preparatory School for lower, middle, and upper school.

During high school, Jared engaged in several activities. He competed on the Lake Highland Congressional Debate team. His senior year, he served as Editor-in-Chief of the award-winning Lake Highland Upper School Newspaper *Twice-Told Tale*. Jared played on the Varsity Men's Volleyball team and Bowling team (although he would hardly call it playing). In addition, he was involved with Investment Club and Student Government, serving as co-president and president of the 12th grade, respectively. Outside of school, Jared volunteered as juror and clerk for Teen Court of the Ninth Judicial Circuit Court of Florida, a voluntary diversionary program from Juvenile Court or school suspension. Prior to attending Notre Dame, Jared interned for the real estate brokerage firm, Kelly Price & Company.

At Notre Dame, Jared is involved with a few activities outside the classroom. He is a member of Student International Business Council, a business organization focused on developing the principles taught in business classes and applying them to useful information pertinent to several divisions of business. He has also travelled on SIBC project teams to Chicago to present pitches to firms. Jared currently serves as the finance director for BridgeND, a chapter of BridgeUSA, which is a bipartisan organization that seeks to bridge the partisan divide among individuals, specifically students. Jared has an interest in the finance industry and is seeking opportunities to work in Investment Banking among other sectors of finance.

His summer after his freshman year at Notre Dame, Jared studied Modern European Politics at the Einaudi Foundation in Torino, Italy, a program through Cornell University. That summer, Jared also interned at the corporate office of International Assets Advisory, a full-service broker dealer and money management firm. He served under the Transitions and Operations team and dealt with compliance-related tasks among other responsibilities.

For fun, he likes to spend time with his roommates and other friends and, should the ever-present permacloud above South Bend dissipate for just a few hours, enjoys frisbee on the quad.

You can connect with Jared at:
- jared.pino@me.com
- www.facebook.com/jared.pino.3
- www.linkedin.com/in/jared-pino

CHAPTER 7

THE P'S TO WINNING

BY JEFF RAMEY

In 1975, in what many consider the greatest World Series ever played, I watched my home state Cincinnati Reds win the World Series over the Boston Red Sox. Like many Reds fans across the country, I sat glued to the TV as George Foster caught the final out off the bat of Carl Yastrzemski. Immediately after the catch was firmly secured by Foster, Johnny Bench ran into Will McEnaney's arms as player after player joined in the celebratory dog pile between pitcher's mound and home plate. As jubilant Reds fans poured from the stands on to the field, the players quickly sought cover in the comforts of their clubhouse.

Once there, they continued their celebration by dousing each other with champagne. Players and coaches hugged one another with tears of joy streaming down their cheeks as each one took their turn hoisting the World Series trophy. All the while, preparations were already being made for a ticker tape parade so that fans could show their appreciation and partake in the celebration. This is the picture of winning that is painted for the average fan. Winning to most means trophies, banners, and ticker tape parades. However, I am not your average fan.

In 1992, I was drafted by those same Cincinnati Reds who I had rooted for since I was a child. While I never had the good fortune of celebrating a World Series Championship, I was a part of two Minor League Championship teams that gave me a microcosm of the World Series celebration I witnessed in 1975. While I took part in dog piles similar to the one I watched on TV and got two Championship rings to display in my trophy case, winning those championships made me realize that winning is much more than trophies, banners, and ticker tape parades. Those things are nice but, are only the rewards of winning. From my championship experiences, winning teams are a collection of players and coaches that have the following winning attitudes and behaviors:

- Positive mindset
- Poise
- Personal sacrifice
- Perseverance
- Powerful leadership
- Preparation

1. Positive Mindset

I have seen time and time again the power of a positive mindset. One example of this was in 1992, shortly after I'd been drafted by the Cincinnati Reds. Following a brief two-week mini spring training in Billings, Montana, we loaded the bus for our first professional games against the Dodgers in Great Falls, Montana. Our nervous energy and butterfly-filled bellies made any chance of sleeping an impossibility. The four-hour bus ride was filled with conversation, movies, card games, and plenty of friendly banter and tomfoolery. At some point, the question arose, "What are you going to do if you don't make it to the major leagues?" A large majority of us answered the question, me included.

At the time, I didn't think much of it but, as time has gone on, I think about two things. First of all, who initiated the question? I'm not going to share the name of the player who started the conversation, but what I am going to tell you is that he didn't make it to the major leagues. Secondly, I think about the three players who I specifically remember not answering the question: Chad Mottola, Tim Belk and Eric Owens. All three of them went on to play in the big leagues. I now know why they sat there in silence. I truly believe that *they weren't going to let any negative thoughts creep into their minds.* Their mindset was that they had been successful and they were going to continue being successful all the way to "The Show."

2. Poise

In 1992, I was in my junior year at Indiana University and we were down four runs in the seventh as we prepared for our final at bat against the University of Michigan. The fourth hitter due up that inning was our All-American shortstop Mike ("Smitty") Smith. "Smitty" was in the midst's of one of the finest seasons in the history of college baseball and is still to this day the only player in Division I baseball history to win the Triple Crown.

As the three hitters before him prepared to bat, he told each one of us, "If you guys get on, I'll tie this thing up!" After a hit and two base-on-balls, "Smitty" came to the plate with an opportunity to back up his words. After two quick strikes by Michigan's All-Big Ten closer Todd Marion, things were looking bleak. However, after stepping out of the batter's box to regain his *composure*, he stepped back in the box and launched the next pitch over the left field fence for a grand slam that sent the game into extra innings. Even though we would win the game in the ninth on my game winning RBI single, there was no doubt that Mike Smith was the true star of the game.

3. Personal Sacrifice

In 1966, Dennis Hegarty was a walk on at Miami-Dade Community College. Legendary Miami-Dade baseball coach Demie Mainieri described Hegarty as "showing no natural tools to play college baseball." He even tried to get Hegarty to quit the team as he saw no possible way that he would ever see the field. However, an injury to the starting left fielder during the Florida State Junior College Tournament forced Hegarty to play. He not only played but played well, even hitting a game winning home run off future major leaguer Gary Gentry in the Junior College World Series. In 1967, the player Hegarty replaced, Preston Pratt, was healthy and ready to reclaim his starting position. However, despite his superior talent, his reluctance to follow the rules forced Coach Mainieri to remove him from the team.

The next morning, following Pratt's dismissal, several players including Dennis Hegarty showed up in Coach Mainieri's office. The players pleaded for him to reinstate Pratt to the team. They felt that not only could Pratt help them win but by keeping him on the team it could also help Pratt mature. *When Coach Mainieri asked Hegarty if he realized that reinstating Pratt to the team would cost him his starting spot, he said yes but, thought it was for the betterment of the team and Pratt.* Pratt was reinstated but never truly lived up to his potential as a baseball player. Dennis Hegarty, on the other hand, would go on to play at Ohio University along side future Hall-of-Famer Mike Schmidt, leading them to the 1970 College World Series. Following his playing career, he became a Hall of Fame high school baseball coach in my hometown of Portsmouth, Ohio.

4. Perseverance

When I think of perseverance I think of my former professional teammate James Lofton. At 5'9" and 160 lbs., the fact that he was even drafted by the Cincinnati Reds was a surprise to many. While I thought he was a solid player, I too had my doubts about his ability to play in the major leagues. After hitting a combined .247 in four seasons in

Class A ball, the Reds had their doubts as well, and gave him his unconditional release. For many, this would have been the end of their baseball career and the beginning of a career in the real world. However, James wasn't quite ready for the real world and signed on with the independent league, Tri-City Posse.

If you are not familiar with the world of independent baseball, this is the bottom rung of professional baseball. Independent leagues have no affiliation with Major League Baseball. It essentially means that your baseball career is on life support. After four seasons in the independent leagues and a solid .293 batting average, James was signed by the Boston Red Sox organization. For most, simply getting signed by a major league organization would have been vindication enough, but for James, his journey wasn't complete. After hitting .315 in 29 games at Double A, he received a promotion to Boston's Triple A affiliate, the Pawtucket Red Sox, one step from the major leagues. Then after hitting .318 in 42 games at Pawtucket, the diminutive, once-released, long shot James Lofton, was called up to the big leagues to start at shortstop for the Boston Red Sox!

When others said no, he said yes. When others said you're too small, he said I'm big enough. When others said quit, he said 'continue on.' And because of his perseverance, he will always be known as James Lofton, the former Big Leaguer!

5. Powerful Leadership

Unless you've shopped for a car in Huntington, West Virginia you've probably never heard the name Lance Daniels. However, of all my former teammates, none exemplified powerful leadership more than he did. This was never more evident than prior to the opening game of our senior year. After leaving the bitter cold of Ohio behind, we traveled to Florida to open our season against Vero Beach High School.

With no outdoor practices or games under our belt, we knew that facing a top ten team from Florida, with an impressive 16-4 record, would be a tough task. Following our pre-game batting practice, our head coach, John Tipton, gathered us down the left field line for some words of encouragement... so we thought.

Instead, he essentially told us to do our best but, the fact that they'd already played twenty games was going to be too much of an obstacle to overcome. Even though I was stunned by his lack of faith, I followed the pack as we began to jog back to the dugout. However, there was one player that never moved from the left field line. As we approached the dugout, we heard Lance Daniels instruct us all to "get back here." As we turned and jogged back, he gathered us in a circle just as Coach Tipton had done moments earlier. However, he delivered a much different message. He basically told us to forget what we'd just heard and to go out there and "kick their A**!" And that is exactly what we did. I have to believe that if Lance Daniels would have joined the pack and jogged back to the dugout following our coaches' pre-game speech; we would not have won that game. But because he didn't, we not only pulled off the upset but, went on to have a very successful season. Lance Daniel's powerful leadership had a lot to do with that.

6. Preparation

Just weeks into my career as a nurse practitioner, I sat in my office searching for the right words to say. A patient in his early 50's had come to see me the week prior complaining of a chronic cough. After trying a course of antibiotics and seeing no improvement in his symptoms, I decided to order a chest X-ray. Then, when the chest X-ray came back abnormal, I ordered a CAT scan of his chest to further evaluate the abnormality. The results of the CAT scan showed he had lung cancer. And not just lung cancer but, small cell lung cancer, the most aggressive type. With his son and wife waiting by his side, I prayed for the right words to say as I got ready to inform them that their father and husband would probably die in less than a year.

If there was ever a situation that I needed poise, this was it. If there was ever a moment that I needed to demonstrate powerful leadership, this was the moment. And if there was ever a time that I needed to encourage a positive mindset and perseverance, this was the time. I can't remember the exact words I said that day but, I do remember leaving the room thinking that I had handled myself well. I got some confirmation of this several months later when the family sent me a card thanking me for my compassion and care.

Since that time, I've had many more similar conversations. This is the reality of my life today. I no longer prepare to hit 95 mile-per-hour fastballs but, instead I have to be prepared to make decisions on a daily basis that impact people's health and potentially their lives. The "game" I'm playing today is much more important. But what I have found is that the recipe for winning in sports is the same as for winning in life. And for this reason, even though my baseball career has long been over, my will to prepare to win has carried on. While there may be some that questioned my ability as a baseball player, I hope that no one questioned my will to prepare. It was because of my will to prepare and the will of my teammates, that I was able to be a part of many winning teams. And with the winning came many awards, but the greatest award is that by preparing to win in the game of baseball, baseball prepared me to win in the game of life.

About Jeff

Jeff Ramey, MSN, APRN is a father, husband and entrepreneur. A former Most Valuable Player during his professional baseball career, he has been a Nurse Practitioner for the past 12 years in his hometown of Portsmouth, Ohio.

Jeff has been featured on countless media outlets, authored a previous book on baseball, and also served as an Adjunct Professor at Ohio University. Ramey resides in Portsmouth, Ohio with his wife, Lara, and his daughters, Olivia and Katie.

CHAPTER 8

PROBLEM SOLVING IN A MODERN WORLD

BY JOHN CRAWFORD

INTRODUCTION

Problems have existed since the dawn of man. They come in all shapes and sizes and usually occur at a high frequency in our lives. Hopefully, in this chapter I will be able to help you understand the basic concepts to problem-solving approaches that will give you the confidence to take on your most difficult problems.

THE REAL PROBLEM

Identifying problems is the first key step to solvability. Sometimes problems can appear simple only to find out they are completely different from what you expected. When trying to identify the problem, you should look for how the problem is manifesting itself. You also have to understand the factors of the problem. Are there other people involved? Many times, other people may view the same problem differently, with a different idea of what would be the best solution outcome. What are the possible solutions and what new problems might those solutions pose? Many times,

when solving a problem, you introduce new problems that may
be worse than the initial problem.

DO YOU AVOID YOUR PROBLEMS?

We have all done some type of problem avoidance. For some
reason many of us feel that if we avoid a problem it will either
go away on its own, or we will never have to actually deal with
it. Sadly, neither of those things ever comes true. If you have
a problem that goes away without interaction, then the truth is
that you never had a problem to begin with. And if you expect a
problem not to affect you while you ignore it, you are most likely
letting it grow until the problem may become so large that your
only resolutions are the "worst case issues", or those that you
wished to avoid in the first place. Avoiding a problem can lead
to the problem taking over your life as you begin changing all of
the things that you do to keep out of the path of the problem. I am
not saying that a problem should be attacked at the first sign that
something is wrong. However, you should start your resolution
process as quickly as possible to avoid the pain that comes from
ignoring it.

Let's take a look at an example problem. Let's say you are given a
task to solve a shipping problem where the shipment was supposed
to go out on Wednesday and arrive on Monday. However, today
is Friday and you are just getting ready to leave for the weekend.
In this case, it could take just a few minutes to come up with a
solution by expediting the shipment for delivery on Monday, and
you may have to stay a little bit longer to ensure that the shipment
is properly sent. And of course, in this simplified example, the
cost of ignoring the problem would be a failure to get the shipment
to the customer on the promised deliver date. This could spawn
even bigger problems including the loss of the order, loss of the
customer or loss of your job. None of the outcomes were probably
worth the inconvenience of staying a little late.

THE BREAKDOWN

Let's face it, one of the reasons we try to avoid problems in the first place is because they feel too big to solve on our own. We get that 100-yard stare just hoping the problem isn't actually there.

A key step in tackling larger problems is breaking them down into smaller problems and solving them individually. This can sometimes be simple or very difficult in its own right, but in either case you will generally have an easier time solving multiple small problems than just trying to think of the big solutions and solving everything at once.

Let's look at a quick example to illustrate how breaking down problems may make your life a whole lot easier. You manage an assembly line that produces a completed product like a clock. And let's say that you're not producing your quotas and are unable to fulfill your orders. There could be several things causing this slow down, and understanding and fixing each of them is the key to getting the main problem solved. You may find that there are not enough workers able to fill all of the spots on the assembly line, or maybe you are not getting your parts on a timely basis, or there are quality control problems with machines that are causing a high number of rejected devices. All of these potential problems could be solved individually and as you solve each one, you end up with a feeling of accomplishment that will help carry you through the next problem.

UNDERSTANDING IS THE KEY

Another setback to solving problems is human interaction. I have spent many days solving a problem that was given to me in an email with all of the information I thought I needed to find the solution—only to discover that each of the stake holders found some issue with my solution making the resolution worthless. When you work on problems that affect multiple people, you will need to work with everyone to make sure you know their pain points in the problem. Otherwise, you may inadvertently make their problem worse.

Being a successful problem solver many times requires being able to understand human personalities. Many large problems will have multiple solutions that you will have to carefully weave through the different personalities of the stakeholders to keep as many people happy as possible. Sometimes, you will undoubtedly be unable to give everyone what he or she wants. When this happens, you may have to work with the highest-level stakeholder or try working with the most forgiving stakeholder – who may take less than their needs in order to get the solution completed.

CALL IN REINFORCEMENTS

Sometimes the fastest and best way to tackle a problem is to get help. Calling in a friend or colleague is not a sign of weakness. Just don't call in people expecting them to do all the work. Not only can another person add perspective, but they also may have knowledge that can help remove a barrier that makes the rest of the problem easier to get through. When it comes to problems, there is usually strength in numbers.

OUTCOME TREES

Organizing around a problem will make your chances at success greatly enhanced. Especially on large problems, you will need to document all of the known aspects of a problem before trying to tackle it. Otherwise, you may run circles and waste time wandering down the same rabbit hole multiple times. One of the best ways to organize around a problem is to use outcome trees. This allows you to test all of the solutions before executing a solution. Outcome trees can also be designed to allow you to catalogue the different factors of a problem and give you a visual insight of the stakeholders, and more importantly, their individual goals. Having this valuable tool in place is a key to successful problem solving.

CONFIDENCE = WIN (OR WINNING)

The impossible problem is the one you never try to solve. You should always enter a problem with the attitude that you are going to solve it. I remember a time with the CEO of a company asking about his laptop, which needed a few updates on it. The technician had called me into his work area because the system had just stopped coming on. At the moment the tech finished explaining this, the CEO stepped into the room and asked when his laptop would be finished. I looked at him and told him we were just about there and would have it to him in about 15 min. I looked at the tech who at that very minute turned completely white and after the CEO stepped out of the room I told him an important secret. I knew we could fix this problem.

I quickly set in motion a quick list of possible issues and resolutions and we started knocking them off the list. After the third possible solution, the system came back on, and after verifying the laptop was updated and fully functional, we happily walked it out to the CIO who proudly gave it to his boss – who thanked us for taking care of it.

If I had panicked and said that there was a much bigger problem, even if we had fixed that problem, there would still be doubt about our ability to solve problems and I would have only reinforced my own doubt as to whether or not I could solve the issue. Instead, I stayed confident that I had the appropriate skills and support to calmly devise the plan needed to tackle the problem, and at the end, everyone had a positive reaction. Going into a problem with confidence will help you chip away at some of the roadblocks your own mind will throw at you.

In the end, devising and following a good plan can help anyone tackle the most difficult problems and solve them in the most efficient and effective manner!

About John

John Crawford has over 20 years of experience solving problems for large Fortune 500 companies and government agencies down to small businesses and non-profits. John has helped many of these organizations identify problems and create new processes and controls to prevent new problems from occurring. During his career, he is constantly refining his approach to troubleshooting and problem solving.

John helped found VADA Solutions LLC, where he currently consults to several large government agencies, and is currently working on bringing his problem-solving approaches to small and medium businesses.

John has a passion for travel and exploration that takes him around the word in search of new adventure.

For additional information, contact:
- media@vadasolutions.com

CHAPTER 9

WINNING THE DAY

BY PATRICK JONES

There I was with my stomach full of food sitting in the movie theatre. I had just stuffed myself with Burger King® and $20 worth of burgers and fries in less than 10 minutes. Now, I am in the movie theatre hoping nobody can hear me sneak in with a bag full of more food. Very slowly and quietly, I go into my backpack and find a bag of M&M's® and a large bag of Skittles®. Within minutes, I binge eat on both bags and I can't feel my stomach to the point that it hurts. I reach into the backpack again, and nothing else is there. The self-hatred began to build up and I am no longer interested in the movie and focus on getting this food out of my body before it's too late.

I quietly got out of my seat only to see the various candies and junk food fall off my lap and on to the ground. I didn't care, I just wanted to get rid of the bad feeling I felt. I walked over to the bathroom and found myself looking in the mirror and asking myself, *"What have I done? I can't even recognize myself."*

The closer I got to the toilet, more intense thoughts about myself poured into my head:
- "You're not a good enough dad."
- "What kind of dad leaves his kids and binges and purges while they sleep?"

- "You are not good enough"
- "This will never end."

I put fingers down my throat and threw up my food to stop the impulsive thoughts and to release the feelings inside. The angrier I was at myself, the harder I vomited. I continued to vomit until nothing was left and my body was empty.

I left the bathroom, praying that nobody heard me and ready to binge on the next thing I could find, only to purge it up again.

This was my life for 15 years. Day after day, night after night, I binged and purged up to five times per day. Nobody knew about it and I felt alone. I left my five kids after they went to bed, and it was a feast and famine and the monster was out of his cage.

In late February 2016, my life changed when I entered rehab to change my life forever. Before I got recovered, I felt defeated. I felt like I could never get ahead and I had this black or white mentality. It was either I was eating perfectly or I was binge eating like crazy. If I ate a carb when I wasn't supposed to, I cheated and just binged the rest of the day.

I wanted to win the day again. I came to a realization in mid 2016. I was already coaching and teaching people healthy habits of nutrition and exercise for the last 15 years, but I was not practicing what I was teaching – which led me to binge eat and shame.

My thoughts started to shift to winning the day. Winning the day in all areas of my life. But specifically with my nutrition and exercise, the two things I could control.

What if I could commit to just winning the day without the obsessive thoughts on food and just focus on accomplishing one thing in my health? Not focusing on some 30- or 60-day goal, or even planning ahead for the next week.

I came to realize all I really had was today. Yesterday is gone and I don't know if tomorrow will even come. If I could just focus on winning the day today, in my health, then I can build momentum and new health habits without focusing on a goal attached to them.

It didn't happen automatically and I did not execute it perfectly. After all, "being perfect" was the route to my eating disorder pattern. Every day I started to ask myself better questions. "What can I do for my health today to win the day?" All I had was today and being present with myself was the key.

In my nutrition recently, I have added a green smoothie to my diet each day, or at least, most days that I am able. In the beginning, I was actually buying the ingredients for the green smoothie and blending them up in my blender. But I kept missing some days here and there, and wasn't winning the day in my nutrition. I found myself not having time to blend it all together. The story in my head kept playing and saying, "the only way I can get a green smoothie in was to blend it." Then, what would happen is if I didn't have time to blend it I wouldn't have a green smoothie that day.

I couldn't win the day in my nutrition with that story. I had to course correct and find a new solution. . . Green smoothie powder! It worked and I am able to use it wherever I go.

I started to notice that when I committed to winning the day with one thing in my nutrition and one thing in my body, things fell into place more easily. Why? Because I did exactly what I said I was going to do! This gave me power, focus and a new sense of energy. All this helped me become more present for my five kids and to create authenticity in my business. Ultimately, I could finally feel happy about myself.

BE THE SNAIL AND WIN THE RACE

I ask my clients this question when we start:

What is one thing you can do TODAY in your nutrition that will help make you healthier or get you closer to your goal?

If you wake up every single morning and stop for thirty seconds and ask yourself this powerful question, it has the power to change your life. The challenge is that most people look at their goal as a long process, and 95% give up halfway through because they lose motivation. By asking yourself this question every single morning, writing down your answer and taking action on the simplest form of the answer, you'll find yourself reaching levels of success in your health, fitness and wellbeing ten times greater than others around you.

Others may reach their "goals" faster, but you'll lap them over and over again when they quit after they stop the diet or weight-loss program. It's like the snail winning the race. The snail will absolutely go slow, but it does not stop, is consistent and will win the race after the cheetah gets too tired, quits and gives up.

My wish for you? Right now, throw away all the diet books, stop clicking on the diet ads and joining weight-loss challenges and detoxes, and start winning the day one health habit at a time!

LIVING THE BINGE-FREE LIFESTYLE

After leaving rehab for 30 days I came back and life was challenging. I was rebirthed and was an entirely new person. For 15 years prior, all I knew was that every problem or feeling I had, I used food to cope with. Now I had to deal with real life issues and I had to find my purpose again.

It took another 12 months before I could really understand myself and how to live in a way that kept me happy, healthy and free from binging and purging. I wanted to spread my message and story to help others struggling, so I created a podcast in mid-2017 and called it The Binge-Free Dad. I wasn't sure why I even called it that until one day, after recording episode #2, it hit me. Binge-Free didn't mean I was never going to binge again. That is what all the binge-eating experts and weight-loss doctors preach: *"I will teach you how to stop binging forever."*

Realistically it's not possible to stop any behavior forever, because you never know if it will come back now or when and how. At that moment, I had realized why the dozens of hours of trying to work the 12-step program Overeaters Anonymous actually made me binge more. In that program, the way it worked was that if I overate or binged in the program, then I screwed up and lost my recovery days and started back to ZERO. It only led me to feel ashamed, and it just led me to binge harder. I wanted to stop binge eating, create a better relationship with food and heal, but I knew there was another way.

So I realized at that moment that the binge-free lifestyle is what I was actually living, right now. It's not thinking "black or white" and I was never going to go back to ZERO if I messed up.

This binge-free lifestyle I created is what keeps me happy, healthy and recovered from my 15-year eating disorder battle. What is this lifestyle exactly? It's a way of living that shatters perfectionism. You live in a way where you let go of it. If you miss a workout, so what, do it the next day. If you ate a carb at 10pm at night and it's not part of your diet, oh well! You didn't cheat on some diet you were on and you don't need to binge eat because of it. You are not restricting your food in the hope to lose weight.

Living the binge-free lifestyle means you are a normal eater and don't plan massive binge episodes. You can easily leave food on your plate and stop eating whenever you want. You can let go of the obsessive food thoughts that you may be attached to. Living this lifestyle means you may skip breakfast just like anyone else and it's ok.

You may binge-eat on occasion, overeat because it's a holiday or stress eat because you just got in a fight with your wife! It is all 100% what normal people do, and is part of living a normal life! You understand there is an abundance of food and that one cookie is enough for now and if you want another, you can have one later! Food no longer controls your thoughts every day. You don't have to "hit the gym" or starve yourself the next day just because you messed up on your diet. You are not scared to eat certain foods, and you have no problem not eating your entire meal at a restaurant and taking some food to go!

THIS IS LIVING THE BINGE-FREE LIFESTYLE!

WINNING THE DAY WITH YOUR NUTRITION

For you, winning the day in your nutrition could be as simple as waking up each morning and eating breakfast within 30 minutes. That alone can shift your metabolism and you could see more energy at work and be more productive. Maybe you find yourself getting through the day without grabbing that candy bar in the afternoon. The crazy part about it is that most diets tell you to remove the candy bar out of the diet right away to lose weight. I stopped telling my clients to remove things years ago because it never worked. Removing things from the diet always had the person crave that food even more!

Here are a few other things you can do today to start winning the day with your nutrition.

1. Add one serving of veggies to your diet
2. Drink 12oz. of water right when you wake up
3. Eat protein first (before you eat the carbs)
4. Add one apple a day into your diet

WINNING THE DAY WITH YOUR BODY

I didn't love my body for so many years. I went up and down in weight because of the binging and purging and chronic dieting. I knew every day I had to do a positive self-love act for my body that I could easily do.

For me, it was getting a workout in each day. I would aim for seven workouts but settle with five as the "non-negotiable" number. Even if it's a quick 7-minute circuit with just my bodyweight in my basement, I would make sure I got it done. Moving my body gives me power and energy and makes me feel good about myself. It also tells my body that I love and respect it no matter what it looks like. For you, it is ok to smart small to win your day with your body. It could be movement, or it could be an act of self-love!

Here are a few ideas for to win the day in your body.

1. Do a plank every morning for as long as you can.
2. Go to the gym if that works for you.
3. Do squats for 60 seconds.
4. Look at yourself in the mirror naked and compliment your body.
5. Walk 15 minutes outside.

See how simple these are? Yes it could be more, or it could be even less. The idea is to start somewhere and build that momentum and healthier habits. If you are getting it now, winning the day in your nutrition and body is about the small things. It's not about going big and going after the giant weight-loss goal. That will come, but you need to build a foundation.

Winning the day, every day, in your nutrition and body will build you up as a person. It will build more and more confidence, momentum and self-love. You begin to be unrecognizable in so many ways. *When you focus on what you can do today to improve your health and take action, you will win the day.*

About Patrick

Patrick Jones is a health and wellness consultant, dad of five kids, and owner of Reshape Corporate Wellness. He is one of the nation's leading experts on inspiring individuals to take control of their health through nutrition and exercise. He hosts the top-rated podcast, *The Binge-Free Dad Show*, where he shares his passion of health and past struggles of binge-eating with the world.

Patrick is a licensed nutritionist and certified eating psychology practitioner and nationally-known expert in the area of food and our relationship with it. He has been a certified personal trainer for almost two decades, a certified reiki master practitioner, and trained as a 200-hour yoga teacher since 2011.

Patrick is known for his energetic passion and engaging speaking-ability in front of large audiences. He has consulted with *Fortune 500* companies on how to create a healthier culture in companies, sharing his powerful story of how he overcame a 15-year addiction of an eating disorder (bulimia and binge-eating up to five times per day). He now teaches individuals what he calls the binge-free lifestyle – happy, healthy and free.

Patrick has been a guest on several nationally-recognized shows on Bravo, MTV, NBC, ABC and Dr. Oz. He has been a 'guest expert' numerous times on CT News 12 television news segments, and is a published writer, having written several articles on health, fitness and nutrition.

In 2004, Patrick was chosen out of 10,000 personal trainers as a finalist in the first ever, personal training apprentice hunt to mentor with the legendary Phil Kaplan. In 2012, he co-hosted a five day per week radio show, *Fit You*, on the world's first fitness radio, with over 80,000 listeners. Patrick is dedicated to helping companies create successful ROI-driven corporate wellness programs and to helping individuals achieve their best self through nutrition and exercise.

You can learn more about Patrick and his programs at:

- BingeFreeDad.com
- ReshapeCorporateWellness.com

CHAPTER 10

THE FIVE RULES OF REAL BUSINESS SUCCESS

BY PAT RIGSBY

All too often we spend our time on day to day things or working on the tactical level without spending much time on stepping back and working on our business.

THE FIVE RULES OF LASTING BUSINESS SUCCESS

Rule #1: Get Clear

Now, I used to think that 'getting clear' meant determining how many clients you wanted, how much revenue you planned to generate or even how much income you'd personally make. Those can be part of it...but they're not what I'm talking about in its entirety. The thing you need to get clear on is what success looks like to you...what your Ideal Business looks like. A subtle, but important distinction.

What does success look like to you? Do you know? Do you know what your Ideal Business looks like? What do you want your life to look like? What is your professional mission?

You might think on the surface it's to make some money or have a fancy office. Often, we trick ourselves into thinking we're in the business of achieving goals that are actually just steps in the bigger journey. But the reality is you want something more specific, whether you have sat down and deliberately figured it out or not.

Here's mine...

Personally, I am very passionate about helping fellow entrepreneurs build the business and the life that they want to have while doing the same for myself. I talk on the phone to clients constantly working on this. I fly around the country for meetings and conferences to accomplish this...and I'm relentlessly studying to find better ways to accomplish this. This is my mission. This is Ideal for me.

There are two phases to this:

> Phase I: What is your mission...what does the Ideal Business look like for you?

Here are some questions that might help you do this:

- What will you sacrifice to make it your reality?
- What is truly important to you personally and professionally?
- What is the outcome you're dedicated to?

For me, I'm willing to travel away from my family more than I want to in order to reach more entrepreneurs or to learn better ways to serve them. It's important because I know a lot of wonderful business owners make some serious sacrifices to serve their clients. I think being able help the clients you want to and have the income, security and enough freedom to go on vacation or coach your kid's Little League team shouldn't be mutually exclusive.

It's something that I've experienced from both sides – as the burned-out coach, putting in ridiculous hours for low pay and no retirement...and as the entrepreneur who can have a significant impact on the people I want to help while still enjoying a family-friendly lifestyle and an income that matches the impact I have.

People are going to doubt you; they're going to try to kill your dreams. You're going to try things and they won't succeed like you planned. What's going to keep you going? It's that Mission, it's your Ideal Business and all that it yields. So, get clear on it! When you're clear on where you're going, lots of other things just fall into place automatically.

Phase II: Why is it so important?

My mission is important to me because I feel that 98% of entrepreneurs settle in life. They settle for less than they are capable of...less than they deserve.

They get up early every day, hustle into work, help dozens... even hundreds of other people reach their goals, enjoy a better, richer, more fulfilling life...all while barely making ends meet, sacrificing time with their family, failing to save money for the future, accepting that a large percentage of the people they serve will be people they don't enjoy – simply because they have to pay the bills; rarely, if ever, taking a vacation; not having time for their family or their own personal interests—all this on the path to burnout or exhaustion. Their only solace is that they get to have their own business, even if it doesn't at all resemble what they originally set out to build.

It's important, because I don't want that for you, and won't accept that for myself. So that's my "why," and I can't stand idly by and have the knowledge of how to overcome that and not share it with fellow trainers and coaches.

It's important to understand your "why" as you think about what you want your Mission and your Ideal Business to look like; my 'whys' are my family and to help other entrepreneurs.

Along with the clarity that you have when you discover where you want to go and the "why" behind it – you'll gain the conviction and the drive to do all that is necessary for lasting success. Because I can assure you, lasting business success takes a tremendous amount of work, but if you're clear on where you're going, it doesn't feel like work at all. Writing the daily email I write...coaching the entrepreneurs I work with...they don't feel much like work at all.

Now I'm not saying that some of what you do won't feel like work because it will. But if you have clarity of purpose, clarity of mission, clarity of what success looks like to you...then you'll be excited about what you are doing, because you'll know that it's moving you toward where you want to go and you'll know what sort of impact you're having each and every day.

One more point. . .

You also need to get clear to what you should be doing. For me the three things I should be doing...the things I'm best at and most passionate about are creating, coaching and 'ideation'.

- *Creating opportunities, resources, relationships and content.*

- *Coaching...be it entrepreneurs or baseball players.*

- *Ideation... developing ideas or recognizing opportunities, either for my own business or for others.*

And the higher percentage of my time I invest in those things and the more of the things that fall outside of those areas that I outsource to people whose strengths complement mine...the faster I move toward my Ideal Business, and the happier I am. So, in addition to getting clear about what success looks like to you and what your personal mission is, you also need to get clear about what you personally should be doing.

Rule #2: Work

One of the biggest misconceptions about the concept of building your Ideal Business is that it doesn't require work. Wrong! Anything worth having requires work, no exceptions. But most people, even most business owners, don't do strategic work that will move them to their goals. They substitute busy work and no one ever achieved any great success by spending most of their time on busy work.

If you read this and then just sit around and reflect on what you learned without doing anything, you'll actually lose ground and be farther from your goals because you'll have wasted your time.

We all already know things we could take strategic action on and here's why it's so important in the bigger picture of achieving success. When you do strategic work you have confidence. Action breeds more action. You feel good about yourself and your ability to achieve success.

If you want to feel unstoppable, do something that moves you toward your goals. Play to your strengths and do something specific that moves you toward the business you want. Do it and see what happens. Measure the results. Do it every day.

If not for the immediate results, do it for what happens in your mind when you do it because you go from thinking to doing. You're making progress, no matter how small. Your identity becomes someone who does and it becomes routine. Once it becomes routine, it leads to expansion for more action. And, the only way to achieve lasting success is constant action.

You have more potential that you can probably imagine, but unless that potential is fed by the best beliefs, attitudes, and resources and then followed up by consistent action, it remains untapped. Tony Robbins has a Success Cycle that I think is spot on:

Potential > Action > Results > Beliefs

What happens is you have this potential, and based on that, you take action. Based on the action you take you produce results. Then, based on the results you get, this feeds your beliefs about what you think your potential is. You can impact this cycle positively at any point.

If you feed your mind with new beliefs, you activate your potential for greater results. When you put that potential to the test by taking new actions, you'll get more and better results. This turns into more positive beliefs and attitudes you hold about yourself and your ability to succeed. These new beliefs and attitudes will unleash even more of your potential, leading to better actions, better results, and on and on. This spiral of success builds incredible momentum.

So, if you start taking action, you'll start to get results and this will feed the whole cycle. When you take action, it gives you confidence so when you're confronted with failure or negativity, you can withstand it and not get derailed.

Focus on investing time in work daily that moves you toward your goals, toward your Ideal Business. Plan your day the evening prior and schedule time to work on building the business that you want. If you can schedule time for others, then you can certainly schedule time for you. Start doing at least a little of this work daily and you'll create momentum that will make you virtually unstoppable.

Rule #3: Embrace Simplicity

If you want to achieve your goals and have lasting business success, then you need to simplify things. If you try to make things too complicated, you won't execute them and others won't be able to follow your plan. In fact, if things are too complicated, that leads to overwhelm and paralysis. Sure, you need to make educated decisions...but you can't let the burden of too much – too much information or too much on your task list – slow you down.

As an entrepreneur you have an advantage, if you choose to use it. You are relatively little and can act quickly. You can move much more quickly than bigger, more bureaucratic businesses, but it's up to you.

As a small business owner trying to affect positive change, there's a lot going on. You can't have clutter. You have a choice...you can be overwhelmed and struggle to get your massive list of things done or you can do a few things and be extraordinary at them.

Imagine an airline pilot with all the stuff he's doing also trying to keep track of the latest gizmo or shiny object. He'd be lucky to get off the ground. The drivers in your business are important. Everything matters. So you need to simplify.

In fact, I try to simplify business as much as I can, so here's how I often look at business in a very simplistic, three-step way:

- Step 1 - Lead Generation
- Step 2 - Conversion
- Step 3 - Delivery

Sure – each of those are comprised of various parts, but to keep things simple you can ask yourself each day:

– Did you generate leads?
– Did you sell?
– Did you fulfill or deliver on your promise?

If you lose focus and become distracted by overwhelm, you're not the best version of you in anyway. So, simplify.

Here's another part of simplification and one that's going to sound strange coming from me. Clear out the information overload. You can't study a dozen different 'experts' in business and a dozen in training and actually execute. Pick a couple, learn from them and apply. The others get put on hold for a while. Ignore them. Put them into a folder, or (gasp) unsubscribe. Focus on execution instead of simply gathering information.

Identify your mission – what success looks like to you – and come up with a plan. Then you have to commit to that plan. You can refine the plan or update it, or better yet – simplify it. Then it's time to focus on execution.

Simplicity leads to Clarity. Clarity leads to the ability to take rapid, decisive Action. Anything else will slow or even kill your progress. Keep it simple and take massive action.

Rule #4: Be Bold

Most people lead average lives...because they aren't bold. To achieve anything extraordinary you have to be bold. You have to be willing to get a little uncomfortable and challenge the norms.

Back in my baseball coaching days, I spent my first two seasons playing it safe, doing things the way that everyone else did them and the results were pretty average. But when I was willing to challenge conventional wisdom and approach things differently, that's when we became a Championship program.

Then, to achieve success in my first business, Holly, Tyler and I lived in a basement for a year. This wasn't in my early twenties... I was 33. Something that most others would be unwilling to do. A bold choice.

I could have stayed in coaching baseball. I had job offers at both the collegiate and the professional level, but while that would have been the comfortable option, it wasn't going to get me to the success I was looking for.

And I had a few job opportunities in sales that were certainly 'safer' and more secure. Jobs that would have been more financially rewarding at the time. But again, that wasn't my dream, my mission.

To do anything big, you've got to be bold.

Most recently, moving on from an organization I'd been building for a decade to pursue my Ideal Business and start focusing on a few things that no one else was teaching (and many thought were not possible)—helping you create your Ideal Business…again, it was bold. But with no risk comes no reward.

And you're going to screw things up. You're going to make people mad. You're going to fail. I've done all three more times than I can remember. I've had so many fails that it's nothing more than a bump in the road when it happens now, it's just part of the process.

Professionally, I look back and my first and biggest 'fail' was being forced to resign after a four-year battle with a Vice President of the University where I coached. I'd built a successful program with some really, really meager resources and being the baseball coach was my entire identity. Resigning, or essentially being fired, was crushing. My self-esteem was at an all-time low. But instead of playing it safe and avoiding risks, in an attempt to avoid feeling like a failure again, I took even bolder steps moving forward, recognizing the pain associated with my first big fail was just a knockdown from which I could dust myself off and get back up. Oh…and ten years later that same University held a baseball tournament named after me and also named me the University's Distinguished Alumnus.

Failure is only a bump in the road. It's a test to weed out the uncommitted. Be bold. It's in the moments when you get back up that your fortune is made. That your goals are realized. You will have challenges, struggles and failures. Just deal with it. Accept it. In fact, welcome it and know that overcoming it will separate you from those who are average.

Now, the formula that allows you to do this really goes back to the first step when we clarified what success looks like to you. Because when you have a mission that's truly meaningful to you, that's the only thing that will pull you through all of the inevitable obstacles you're going to encounter along the way. I can assure you, the rewards of being bold outweigh any benefit of playing small. When you're crystal clear, everything else unfolds. You get the willingness, the drive to take action, the ability to make the right decisions and you're able to get past the obstacles in the way.

#5: Everything Matters

What I mean by this is that every single choice or action is either moving us closer to, or farther from, our goals. We're a product of our choices. Our businesses and our lives are reflections of the actions we did or didn't take.

Every day we have the option to plan tomorrow or to simply wake up and react to what comes our way. Every day we choose how we're feeding our mind…what we're reading or learning from. Every day we decide how we're going to engage (or fail to engage) with the people in our lives, from our family and friends to our clients and prospects. We decide if we're going to take specific actions to move toward our goals or put them off until tomorrow.

In truth – we decide whether we believe success is even possible. Our self-talk is often the first domino for many of the choices we'll make.

We decide who we spend our time with, and I'll tell you that if you spend your time with negative people…you're going to be negative. If you surround yourself with others who play small… so will you.

And you don't really get to pick and choose which decisions actually matter. Which choices will be important. You never know how you treat someone on a given day will impact you, your relationship or even your business a year down the road. You never know when the seminar you attend or the book you read will be the one that changes everything.

I've seen people's lives ruined, or even ended, by a poor choice. I've seen people's lives forever improved by a single, seemingly simple choice too. It's a powerful reminder that every little thing we choose affects us. Sometimes we just become so numb to it, we don't realize how powerful of an effect it's really having on us and how we're moving toward or away from our goals. Every single thing matters.

So, in summary, here are *The Five Rules of Lasting Business Success:*

- **Rule #1: Get Clear**
- **Rule #2: Work**
- **Rule #3: Embrace Simplicity**
- **Rule #4: Be Bold**
- **Rule #5: Everything Matters**

They're not tactical. They're not magic bullets or quick fixes. They're the foundation that any success you want to have can and will be built on. Embrace them and virtually any goal you set out to achieve will ultimately be yours

About Pat

In the past decade Pat Rigsby has built over 25 businesses as a CEO and Co-Owner, with five becoming million-dollar or multi-million dollar ventures. Two of those businesses, Athletic Revolution and Fitness Revolution, have been multiple-time winners on the Entrepreneur Franchise 500 with each being the #1 franchise for its respective market. Another business, Fitness Consulting Group, was a multiple time honoree on the Inc. 5000, placing as high as #580 on the list of fastest growing businesses in the U.S. He's also been a Best-Selling Author eleven times over, presented in front of thousands of entrepreneurs, and been featured in *Entrepreneur, Forbes, Men's Health, USA Today* and on hundreds of other media outlets.

When it comes to sales, Pat's personally sold as many as 116 franchises in a single year and been the strategist and copywriter for over 10 million dollars in online sales from his own businesses and millions more in sales for his clients.

Pat's coaching and consulting clients have been featured in places like *Men's Health, USA Today, Men's Fitness, Shape, Women's Health, Huffington Post* and on ABC, CBS, NBC and many other media outlets. In addition to that, they have built some of the most successful businesses and brands in every corner of the industry, from local business and supplement companies to online businesses, certification organizations and even became best-selling authors. In fact, many (if not most) of the experts providing business coaching in the fitness industry have been his clients, customers or franchisees.

And the best part of this? He's been able to do all of these things and more while working from home, coaching his kids in baseball and soccer, and enjoying a type of entrepreneurial lifestyle he would have never thought possible just a few short years ago.

If you'd like to see how you might be able to work together with Pat, you can reach him at:
- pat@patrigsby.com.